The Theatre Student

SOUND AND MUSIC
FOR THE THEATRE

The Theatre Student

SOUND AND MUSIC FOR THE THEATRE

Carol M. Waaser

With Special Chapter by
Gregory Sandow

PUBLISHED BY
RICHARDS ROSEN PRESS, INC.
NEW YORK, N.Y. 10010

Published in 1976 by Richards Rosen Press, Inc.
29 East 21st Street, New York, N.Y. 10010

First Edition

Library of Congress Cataloging in Publication Data

Waaser, Carol M
    The theatre student.

(The Theatre student series)
    Bibliography: p.
    SUMMARY: Explains the techniques of sound engineer-
ing, sound design, and composition for the theater.
    1. Music in theaters.   2.   Theaters—Sound effects.
[1. Music in theaters.   2.   Theaters—Sound effects]
I. Title. II. Title: Sound and music for the theatre.
MT960.W2   620.2'02'4792   75–43694
ISBN 0–8239–0318–4

Manufactured in the United States of America

CAROL M. WAASER holds a bachelor's degree from Wilson College and an M.F.A. degree from the Yale School of Drama. From 1970 to 1975 she held the positions of Resident Stage Manager at the Yale Repertory Theatre and Instructor in Audio Techniques at the Yale Drama School. She served as sound engineer for composer Richard Peaslee on the Yale productions of *The Bacchae* and *Don Juan* and has designed sound for many shows, including the American premieres of Jules Feiffer's *God Bless* and Eugene Ionesco's *Macbett.* Miss Waaser has also worked in the area of designing and building sound systems for the theatre. She is currently free-lancing as a lighting designer, sound designer, and consultant.

GREGORY SANDOW is a free-lance composer and conductor. His most recent work is an opera, *The Fall of the House of Usher,* with libretto by the noted science-fiction writer Thomas Disch. He has written music for many theatrical productions, including the American premiere of Ionesco's *Macbett,* on which he worked closely with Carol Waaser. He holds an M.M. degree in Composition from the Yale School of Music.

CONTENTS

Theatre is a collaborative art; it is the result of many different artists working together to achieve a final production. If that production is to be truly a work of art, the end result must be a unified whole in which the individual parts are not distinguishable as such. That is primarily the job of the director, to conceive a production in which the scenery, the costumes, the acting style, the lights and sound all mold together into a production concept that brings an added dimension to the written script. But it is the job of each individual artist working on the show to make his contribution serve the production rather than to create something that will stand on its own artistically. No matter how beautiful a scene design is, no matter how well constructed, how accurately painted, it is not good unless it works for the production concept of that particular show. The same is true for all the individual elements that make up a theatrical production, including sound and music.

This book is concerned with explaining the techniques of sound engineering, sound design, and composition *for the theatre.* Some of the theories and methods described may not be considered "correct" in a commercial recording studio, but they work for the theatrical sound designer and are therefore included. There are two approaches to a book such as this. One is for the student who already knows something about theatre but knows very little about

sound, the other is for the student who has a previous knowledge of sound techniques but knows little about the theatre. I believe I have leaned more toward the theatre student who wishes to learn about sound than vice versa, although I have tried to include explanations for the beginning student of theatre as well.

A note to the teacher: The order of the chapters is the logical one for a written text. When I teach the course, however, I usually begin with an explanation of the use of equipment and basic recording and editing techniques. It helps to hold the students' interest through some of the theory if they know what the application of the theory will be. They are also better prepared to do lab sessions throughout the course. (Lab sessions include: recording techniques; editing techniques; microphone tests of different types of microphones to determine which to use in each type of recording situation; room ambiance tests; oscilloscope demonstrations of wave forms, amplitude and frequency changes, and modulation patterns; correct wiring procedures; and demonstrations of acoustical and psychoacoustical phenomena usually done in your particular theatre to determine reflection patterns, interference patterns, masking phenomena, threshold level of audibility, level of subconscious awareness, recovery time from auditory fatigue, etc.). The explanations of acoustics, psychoacoustics, and the scientific principles of equipment in this book are necessarily basic, and students are encouraged to do further studies in these subjects. Students are also encouraged to be experimental and creative, but whenever possible their creative energies should be channeled into a production situation as opposed to a theoretical project.

The Theatre Student

*SOUND AND MUSIC
FOR THE THEATRE*

Chapter I

ACOUSTICS

The subject of acoustics is extensive, and many volumes have been written on it alone. The scope of this book will not permit an extensive investigation of acoustics, but several books are listed in the bibliography for those students who wish to study it more thoroughly. I shall try to give a clear description of the properties of sound which must be understood for the proper use of sound equipment and the creation of sound effects. I shall not discuss architectural acoustics in any detail, and I shall avoid the use of complex mathematical formulas whenever possible.

WAVE PROPAGATION

For simplicity let us consider the propagation of sound waves in air of a pressure and density that is normal at sea level and of a moderate temperature and humidity. Changes in these elements affect the manner in which sound travels through air, but these differences are not essential to understanding the basics of sound-wave propagation. The one condition imposed on any medium (solid, liquid, or gas) for it to be capable of propagating sound waves is that it be elastic. The dictionary definition of elastic is "1: springy; 2: flexible, pliable; 3: adaptable."[1] Air is made up of many millions of molecules, closely packed but separated by complex forces that act like tiny springs. If a force is exerted in a certain direction on one molecule, it will move in that direction until the springy cushion between it and the next molecule is compressed to its limit. The energy of that force and motion will then be passed on to the next molecule, causing it to move in the given direction until it has compressed the cushion between it and its next neighboring molecule. This continues, with a minute amount of energy being absorbed or dissipated. Now enlarge your vision of this to include an area of many, many molecules (Fig. I–la). Assume that these molecules are evenly distributed and equidistant. It can then be said that they are of equal density and under equal pressure throughout the area. Let us imagine that this area is actually a tube with a movable piston at one end. If the piston is displaced to the right one inch it will compress those molecules nearest to it (Fig. I–lb). As you can see, the density of those molecules at the left end of the tube has increased, and, as they are compressing to the right, the pressure at the right of the compressed group of molecules has also increased. This increased pressure will compress the next layer of molecules, and the same chain reaction explained above will occur (Fig. I–lc).

If the piston now returns to its original

---

[1] *The New Merriam-Webster Pocket Dictionary,* 1971.

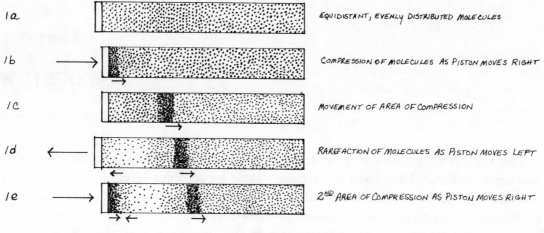

1a   *EQUIDISTANT, EVENLY DISTRIBUTED MOLECULES*

1b   *COMPRESSION OF MOLECULES AS PISTON MOVES RIGHT*

1c   *MOVEMENT OF AREA OF COMPRESSION*

1d   *RAREFACTION OF MOLECULES AS PISTON MOVES LEFT*

1e   *2ND AREA OF COMPRESSION AS PISTON MOVES RIGHT*

Fig. I–1

position (Fig. I–1d), then where there was a compression of molecules there is now a rarefaction. This will cause the molecules nearest the area to accelerate in the reverse direction to fill that space, and the entire process is reversed. Now let us push the piston back in (toward the right) and create another area of compression (Fig. I–1e). In graph form these waves of compression and rarefaction would be expressed as in Figure I–2, with pressure being plotted against time. We have just described in simple terms the laws of linear wave motion. Sound waves travel in accordance with these laws. The linear characteristics of sound waves mean that two or more sounds can travel through the air without interfering with each other. The air can support many different sound waves of different frequencies and different degrees of loudness in a completely independent fashion without interference or distortion. (Certain types of interference and distortion occur within the human hearing mechanism. These are referred to as psy-

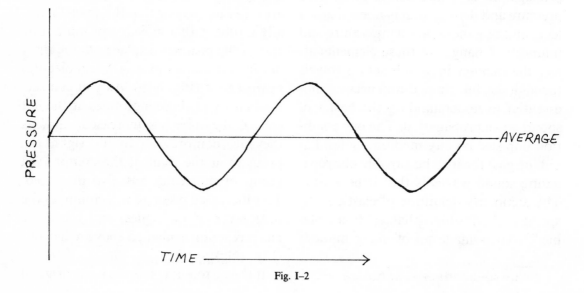

Fig. I–2

choacoustical phenomena and are discussed in Chapter VIII. They should not be confused with the strictly linear characteristics of sound as it travels through the air.) An excellent illustration of the manner in which sound waves behave is a simple *ripple tank.* Any agitation of the water sets up a pattern of ripples or waves that flow across the water. If two sets of ripples are promoted simultaneously they will be seen to flow through each other independently.

Let us return for a moment to the piston in the tube. If the piston moves forward and backward at a constant and regular rate (*f* number of times each second) the wave pattern generated by this motion will be what is known as a sinusoidal or sine wave and will have certain physical and mathematical properties. The wave will go through a complete cycle *f* times a second; it is said to have a frequency of *f* cycles per second (cps). (The term Hertz [Hz] is commonly used as the measuring unit of frequency. One Hz equals one cycle per second.) One complete cycle goes from the peak of one wave to the peak of the next (Fig. I–3), and that distance is said to be one wavelength (denoted by the Greek letter lambda, λ). We know from basic laws of physics that the distance traveled by a moving object is a function of its speed and the length of time it has been moving

at that speed. The velocity or speed of sound in air at room temperature is approximately 1,130 feet per second. If a sound wave has a frequency of *f* cps then the elapsed time from one peak to the next is $\frac{1}{f}$ seconds. So the following equations can be made to express wavelength (λ), frequency (f), and speed (c) of sound:

$$\lambda = \frac{1130}{f} \text{ (expressed in feet)}$$

$$f = \frac{1130}{\lambda} \text{ (expressed in cps or Hz)}$$

So far we have been dealing only with the horizontal axis of the plotted wave. The vertical axis represents pressure or, in terms of the plotted wave, amplitude. A change in volume of a sound is represented graphically by a change in height of the peak of the wave. Figure I–4 shows a comparison of waves of different frequencies and amplitudes.

FREQUENCY, RESONANCE, HARMONICS

The frequency of a tone determines its pitch—the higher the frequency, the higher the pitch. Certain mathematical properties of frequency and pitch are very helpful to us. A tone that is double the frequency of another tone will be one octave higher; a tone that is half the frequency of another tone will be one octave lower. These mathematical properties are important when we investigate such things as standing waves, resonant frequencies, and harmonics. Let us once again consider the tube or pipe through which a sound wave travels from left to

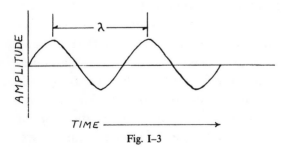

Fig. I–3

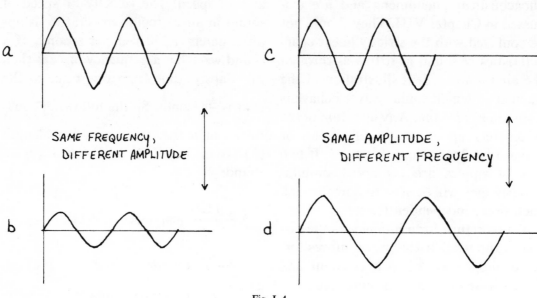

Fig. I–4

right. If the pipe is plugged at the right end, the sound wave will be reflected back from right to left. Since the molecules at the plug cannot move to the right, we know that the total velocity of those molecules (that is, the sum of the velocities of the initial or incident wave and of the reflected wave) must be zero. So the velocity of the reflected wave must be equal and opposite to the velocity of the incident wave. Figure I–5 illustrates the velocities of the two waves at three different times in the cycle. The total velocity is always zero at the plug and also at points of half wavelength increments along the path of the wave.

If we now plug the tube at the left end as well, the wave will again be reflected, this time back to the right. If the length of the wave is mathematically related to the length of the tube, the second reflected wave will combine with and reinforce the incident wave. Any frequency that has a wavelength of a mathematical

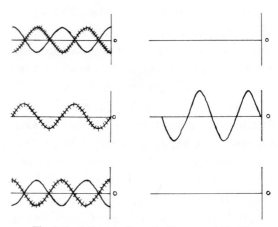

Fig. I–5 *(after van Bergeijk, Pierce, and David)*

relationship to the length of the pipe such that the reflected waves join with and reinforce the incident wave is called a resonant frequency. (The pipe is known as a resonator.) The lowest resonant frequency that can be supported by any resonator is known as the fundamental frequency. For a pipe closed at both ends the fundamental frequency has a wavelength of twice the length of the pipe, or $\lambda = 2L$, and the frequency can be ex-

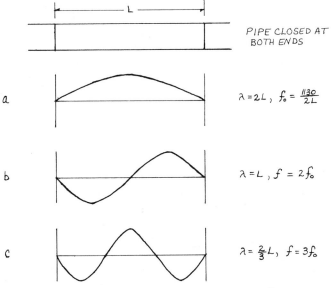

PIPE CLOSED AT BOTH ENDS

a $\lambda = 2L$, $f_0 = \dfrac{1130}{2L}$

b $\lambda = L$, $f = 2f_0$

c $\lambda = \dfrac{2}{3}L$, $f = 3f_0$

Fig. 1–6   *(after van Bergeijk, Pierce, and David)*

pressed: $f_0 = \dfrac{1130}{2L}$ (Fig. I–6). This type of resonator will support all frequencies that are whole-number multiples of the fundamental frequency—$2f_0$, $3f_0$, $4f_0$, etc. These frequencies are known as harmonics of the fundamental frequency: $2f_0$ is the second harmonic and is one octave higher than the fundamental; $3f_0$ is the third harmonic and is musically a fifth above the octave ($2f_0$); $4f_0$ is the fourth harmonic and is the second octave. As you can see, the harmonics are both mathematically and musically related. If we continued up through the harmonic frequencies, we would find that $5f_0$ is the third above the second octave, $6f_0$ is the fifth above the second octave, $7f_0$ is the seventh above the second octave, and $8f_0$ is the third octave. This is shown musically in the scale of Figure I–7.

The mathematical relationship of the wavelength of the fundamental frequency to the length of the pipe will vary depending on whether the ends of the pipe are plugged or unplugged. As we have seen, the wavelength of the fundamental frequency of a pipe that is plugged at both ends is 2L. If a pipe is plugged at the right end but open at the left end (Fig. I–8a), the wavelength of the fundamental frequency is 4L and the

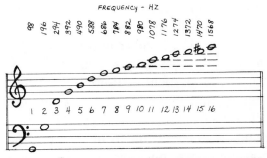

Fig. I–7   *Harmonic scale of fundamental frequency of 98 Hz (after Taylor).*

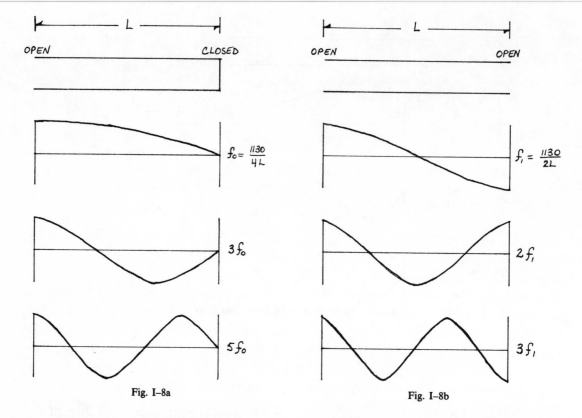

Fig. I–8a

Fig. I–8b

pipe resonates only at the odd harmonics of the fundamental frequency. If the pipe is open at both ends (Fig. I–8b), the wavelength of the fundamental frequency is 2L and the pipe resonates at all harmonics. These differences in the resonant properties of different types of resonators are very important in the design of musical instruments. Most resonators, when supporting one frequency, will also produce, at the same time but to a lesser degree, some harmonic frequencies. These are known as overtones. The number and the strength of the overtones give a musical instrument the particular timbre or sound quality that makes it recognizable and different from any other type of instrument. It is important to understand the concept of overtones and timbre, because this is one of the primary ways we can

distinguish any sound from any other.

It is a property of sine waves that they add in a linear manner; that is, they can be added graphically. This is illustrated in Figure I–9, where curve A represents a wave of frequency f_1 and an amplitude a_1, curve B represents a wave of frequency $3f_1$ and an amplitude $\frac{a_1}{3}$, and curve C represents the sum of waves A and B. As you can see, the shape of the resultant wave is no longer that of a sine wave. If we were to continue to add waves of different frequencies and amplitudes we could build different wave shapes. J. B. J. Fourier, a 19th-century French mathematician, proved a theorem showing that any complex wave form can actually be represented as the sum of sinusoidal waves of different frequencies and amplitudes. Any of the

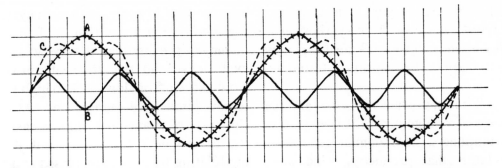

Fig. I–9 *Line A represents a wave of frequency fo and Amplitude A_0. Line B represents a wave of frequency $3f_0$ and amplitude $\frac{1}{3}A_0$. Line C represents the sum of A and B. Use the grid to plot the linear addition of the two waves A and B.*

symmetrical wave forms (such as square waves, triangle waves, and sawtooth waves) can be shown to be the sum of a fundamental wave and certain of its harmonics. The square wave, for instance, is the sum of a fundamental and its odd harmonics (f_0, $3f_0$, $5f_0$, $7f_0$, etc.). The purity or lack of distortion of the wave form is dependent on the amplitudes of the different harmonic frequencies.

If you have the use of an electronic synthesizer and an oscilloscope, it is possible to demonstrate wave forms and their relationships. Connect the outputs of the synthesizer to the oscilloscope (as well as to an amplifier and speaker setup), and watch the shape of the wave on the scope as you listen to the timbre of the sound. Most synthesizers can generate sine waves, square waves, triangle waves, sawtooth waves, and trapezoidal waves (Fig. I–10). Sweep through different frequencies and different amplitudes to show the change in the wave pattern. Then take one of the complex wave forms, put it through a filter, and filter out all the harmonics, leaving just the fundamental sine wave.

While we are on the subject of electronic synthesizers, we should discuss frequency modulation and amplitude modulation. These subjects will concern a sound designer on a practical level only if he has access to a synthesizer (or other

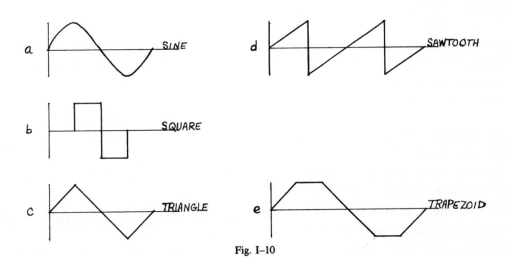

Fig. I–10

voltage-controlled signal generators and amplifiers); but even if no synthesizer is available, the theoretical knowledge may help to clarify other aspects of sound design.

First, it is important to understand the concept of voltage-controlled generators and amplifiers. Most signal generators (oscillators that produce specific wave form signals such as sine or square waves) have manual controls for varying the frequency of the signal. A voltage-controlled generator also has a special input for variable voltage that will automatically vary the frequency of the signal according to the voltage at the input. If the variable voltage at the input of oscillator number 1 is taken from the output of oscillator number 2, the effect will be to vary or modulate the frequency according to the amplitude or shape of wave number 2. Figure I–11 shows a sine

bottom would happen with each cycle of the modulating wave; that is, if the frequency of the modulating wave were one cycle per second, then the resultant wave would sweep from low pitch to high pitch to low pitch once each second. At that slow rate of change it would be easy for the ear to hear the sweep, but if the modulating wave were increased to a frequency of 100 cps, the ear could not distinguish the rapid sweeps up and down but would instead hear several different frequencies, which would sound like a buzz. It is impossible to describe the sound of the resultant waves as the modulating frequency is changed. I suggest that, if possible, you do your own experiments, using an oscilloscope as well as speakers to monitor the output, so that you can see the wave forms as you hear how they sound. Figures I–12 and I–13 show a sine wave modulated by a square wave and a sawtooth wave, respectively. The square wave modulation at a low rate of modulation would sound like a steady pitch at a high frequency, then a steady pitch at a low frequency, with no sweep to get from one to the

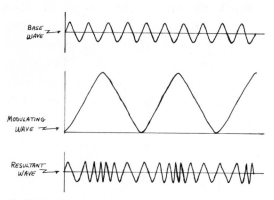

Fig. I–11 *Frequency modulation of one sine wave by another sine wave.*

wave being frequency-modulated by another sine wave. The amplitude of the modulated wave does not change; only the frequency changes. The sound of the resultant signal would be a very even sweeping up and down of the pitch, one complete sweep from bottom to top to

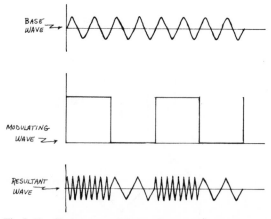

Fig. I–12 *Frequency modulation of sine wave by square wave.*

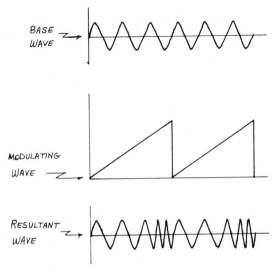

BASE WAVE

MODULATING WAVE

RESULTANT WAVE

Fig. I–13 *Frequency modulation of sine wave by sawtooth wave.*

other, just a sudden transition. The sawtooth wave modulation would sound like a sweep from a low frequency to a high frequency, then a direct drop back to the low frequency for another sweep up.

A voltage-controlled amplifier enables

the amplitude of a wave to be varied automatically, in most cases according to the frequency and shape of another wave. This is illustrated in Figures I–14, I–15, and I–16. In the case of amplitude modulation, only the amplitude, not the frequency, is changed, and the sound will become louder and softer according to the shape of the modulating wave. You will notice that if we draw a smooth curve connecting the peaks of the resultant wave, the outline is the modulating wave form. This outline is also known as the envelope of the sound. We shall discuss sound envelopes more fully a little later. Referring once again to Figure I–14, you will see the outline of the resultant wave. If the frequency of the modulating wave is within the audible spectrum, it will be heard along with the resultant wave. Once again, you should do your own experiments in amplitude

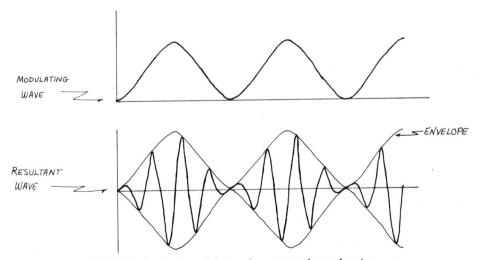

MODULATING WAVE

RESULTANT WAVE

ENVELOPE

Fig. I–14 *Amplitude modulation of a sine wave by another sine wave.*

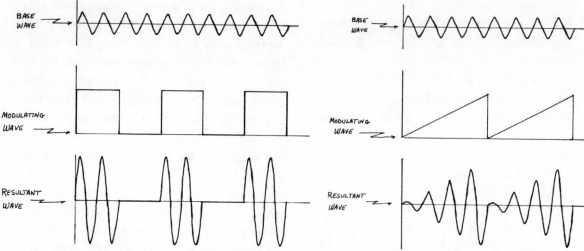

Fig. I–15 *Amplitude modulation of a sine wave by a square wave.*

Fig. I–16 *Amplitude modulation of a sine wave by a sawtooth wave.*

modulation to know the variety of sounds it can produce.

The explanations above describe frequency modulation and amplitude modulation as they are useful in creating sound effects. These are not adequate explanations of the way FM and AM are used in radio broadcast; that information can be obtained from any good radio electronics text.

ENVELOPES, PHASING, AND BEATS

In acoustical matters the term envelope is used in discussing the shape of a wave or of a sound. We have already seen its use in reference to a wave pattern. The outline of an amplitude modulation pattern is known as its envelope (Fig. I–14). The term is also used to describe the amplitude pattern, in respect to time, of an entire sound. A sound envelope has four parts: the attack time, the on time, the decay time, and the off time. A sound is said to have a sharp attack if it begins at its full amplitude or if it ar-

rives at its full amplitude quickly; a sound is said to have a gradual attack if it goes slowly from a low amplitude to its full amplitude. A single beat on a snare drum has a very sharp attack, whereas a siren has a more gradual attack (Fig. I–17). The on time is how long the sound remains at its full amplitude. A single drum beat is instantaneous and has virtually no on time, whereas a siren remains on as long as air is forced through it at a continuous rate. The decay is the time it takes a sound to die

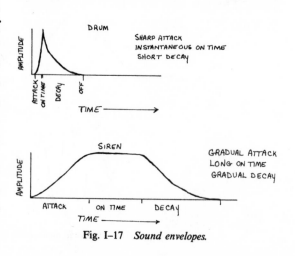

Fig. I–17 *Sound envelopes.*

out. This may differ between electronic measurements and acoustical measurements depending on the reverberation characteristics of the room in which acoustical measurements are made. Most sounds have at least some natural decay, and the off time is an extension of the decay. Some sounds, however, are damped and the natural decay is cut short by a sharp off, such as when a percussionist damps a cymbal crash with his hand (Fig. I–18).

We have now seen that a sound has four aspects: its frequency, which determines its pitch; its amplitude, which determines its volume; its wave form, which determines its timbre or sound quality; and its envelope, which determines its duration. There is one other important consideration in any complex sound (that is, anything more complex than a single, simple sine wave), and that is phasing. As we know, sine waves consist of regular, periodic crests and troughs (Fig. I–19). Phasing is the periodic relationship of any two or more waves; that is, if two waves coincide crest to crest and trough to trough they are said to be in phase. If they do not precisely coincide they are said to be out of phase. The amount by which they do not coincide is the degree to which they are

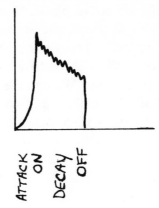

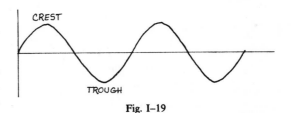

Fig. I–18 *Sound envelope of damped cymbal crash.*

Fig. I–19

out of phase (Fig. I–20). Since sine waves add in a linear manner, we can see that two waves arriving crest with crest and trough with trough (in phase) will add to each other and reinforce each other. Looking at Figure I–20a, we can see that the addition of two identical waves that are 180° out of phase will constantly equal zero; in other words, the two waves will completely cancel each other. Waves that are only partially out of phase will cancel each other only to the degree to

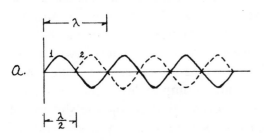

180° OUT OF PHASE - WAVE 2 BEGINS ½ WAVELENGTH LATER THAN WAVE 1.

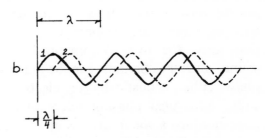

90° OUT OF PHASE - WAVE 2 BEGINS ¼ WAVELENGTH LATER THAN WAVE 1.

Fig. I–20

which they are out of phase. Waves that are 180° out of phase but are not completely identical will only partially cancel each other to the degree to which they resemble each other. We can see the importance of proper phasing if we look at Figure I–21. Both wave patterns are the the walls and ceilings. (Since the reflected waves have a greater distance to travel, they will arrive later than the direct wave.) The amount of delay in the reflected waves will determine the phase differences between the direct wave and the reflected waves. The simplest form of

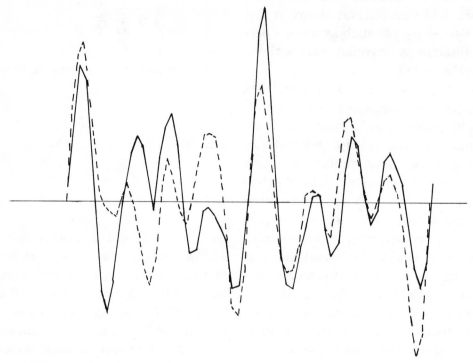

Fig. I–21 *Resultant waves of combining the same five sine waves in different phase relationships.*

combination of the same 5 waves. The only difference between the two combinations is the relative phase of each component wave to the others; the frequencies and amplitudes remain the same. Obviously, the two combinations will sound different. Sounds can be out of phase either acoustically or electronically. Acoustical phasing refers to the time at which a sound arrives at the ear (or microphone). If a sound is propagated in a room, the ear or microphone will receive the direct sound wave first and then receive the reflected waves from

electronic phasing is seen in the wiring of microphones and speakers. If the hot and common leads to one speaker are the reverse of what they are to another speaker, the two speakers will be 180° out of phase. The same is true of two microphones wired the reverse of each other. On a more complex level, there are electronic devices that enable the shifting of phase of a sound to any degree out of phase with itself or another sound.

Another phenomenon associated with acoustical phasing is of interest to the sound designer. Two tones that are close together in frequency have wavelengths that differ only slightly. If they are sounded simultaneously and sustained, the nearly identical waves will start out in phase and reinforce each other, but because the wavelengths are not absolutely identical they will gradually shift more and more out of phase until they are 180° out of phase and almost completely cancel each other (Fig. I–22). Because the frequencies are very close

farther apart, say 300 and 350 Hz, the difference frequency would be 50 Hz; that is, the beats would occur 50 times per second and would not be distinguishable as beats but would be heard as a 50-Hz hum very softly under the initial tones.

MEASURING SOUND

One of the great marvels of the acoustical world is the broad range of sound

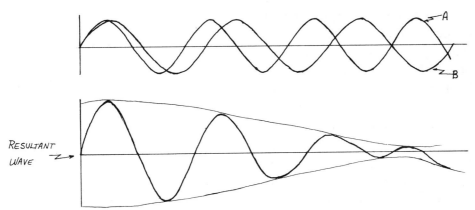

Fig. I–22   *Beats occur when two waves (A and B) are close to but not exactly the same frequency. The envelope of the resultant wave is the difference frequency of A and B.*

together, the ear may not be able to distinguish the two separate pitches, but will hear one tone that will grow louder and softer as the two tones alternately reinforce and cancel each other. This phenomenon is known as "beats." As you can see in Figure I–22, the envelope of the amplitude changes of the resultant wave is similar to that produced by amplitude modulation (Fig. I–14). The frequency of the envelope is the difference between the two initial frequencies; in other words, if the two initial tones were 20 Hz and 21 Hz (two of the lowest notes on a pipe organ), the difference frequency would be 1 Hz. The beats could be easily distinguished at a rate of one per second. If the initial frequencies were higher and

power that can be detected by the human ear. In fact, the loudest sound that the human ear can detect before it becomes painful is more than one hundred billion times louder than the softest sound detectable by the ear. It would be difficult in everyday conversation to discuss sounds in terms of such large figures, so a method was devised to compare sound powers logarithmically to keep the numbers within a reasonable scale. The unit of measure in this method is the decibel (db). Notice that I used the phrase "compare sound powers." Since most of us do not walk around carrying sound meters so that we can state precisely how loud each particular sound is, we tend to judge the loudness of sounds in terms of other sounds; that is, we notice if one sound is louder or softer than another sound. But at what point can we distinguish that one sound is louder than another? If a sound is very soft, another sound does not have to have much more intensity for us to distinguish the difference, but if a sound is very loud, another sound would have to have relatively greater intensity (in terms of real sound power) to have the same noticeable effect of being louder that we found between the soft sounds. (As an experiment, try singing very softly, then increase your volume until you are singing just noticeably louder. This change in volume will not take a great deal more energy. Now sing loudly, then increase the volume until it is noticeably louder. This change in volume will take a great deal more energy to accomplish than the first change, yet the noticeable audible difference should be similar.) This leads us to believe that the just noticeable difference in loudness between two sounds is based on a fraction or percentage rather than on a constant numerical difference. In fact, the German physicist E. H. Weber stated this in 1834. Weber's law stated that a sound stimulus must be increased by a constant fraction of its value to be just noticeably different. Later research showed that this is not precisely true, but it is close enough to make viable a method of sound measurement based on power *ratios* rather than power differences.

The decibel indicates a ratio between two sound powers on a logarithmic scale. If one sound is 10 times as powerful as another, it is 10 db louder. If a sound is 100 times as powerful as another, it is 20 db louder. The table in Figure I–23

Ratio of Powers of Two Sounds	Relationship in Decibels Between the Two Sounds
1	0 db
10	10 db
100	20 db
1000	30 db
10000	40 db
100000	50 db
1,000,000	60 db
10,000,000	70 db
.	.
.	.
.	.
10,000,000,000	100 db
.1	−10 db
.01	−20 db
.001	−30 db
.	.
.	.
.	.
.000001	−60 db
200	23 db
400	26 db
600	27.8 db
800	29 db
1000	30 db
1600	32 db
2000	33 db

Fig. I–23

shows the relationship in decibels of various sound power ratios. Several things become obvious upon studying the table. Without knowing anything about logarithms, it is possible to grasp a functional knowledge of decibels. First of all, in the first section of the table, the number of decibels is always equal to 10 times the number of zeros in the ratio figure. One thousand has 3 zeros in it, so the decibel relationship is 10 × 3, or 30. The second section of the table deals with decimal ratios which indicate that the second sound is less powerful than the first, and therefore the decibel relationship is negative. The number of decibels is equal to 10 times the number of decimal places in the ratio figure. The third section of the table indicates some decibel figures for intermediate ratios. To obtain accurate decibel figures for those numbers, you would have to refer to the formula for computing decibels and the logarithm scale. But approximations can be made using the following guide: if you double the sound power ratio, you increase the decibel figure by 3 db. For those who understand logarithms, the formula for computing the decibel relationship between two sound powers is:

$$\text{INTENSITY LEVEL} = 10 \log_{10} \frac{\text{INTENSITY}_2}{\text{INTENSITY}_1} \qquad \left(\text{IL} = 10 \log_{10} \frac{I_2}{I_1} \right)$$

You will notice that the decibel is always a measurement of the *ratio between two sound powers*. It cannot be used to describe a sound level independent of a reference level. Why, then, do people refer to a rock band as putting out 110 db of sound? It has become standard practice to assign a reference level of 0 db to the sound power that is considered the threshold of hearing in a very healthy ear. This sound power is considered to be 10^{-12} watts/m² or 0.000 000 000 001 watts/m². It is always in reference to this level that a sound is said to be so many decibels loud. Thus, a sound that has an intensity of 80 db above reference has an actual intensity level of 0.0001 watts/m².

You will notice that sound intensity levels are measured in watts *per square meter;* that is, measured in terms of space. Sound waves diminish in intensity as they travel through air. Much of the energy is used up in heat, and some is absorbed by objects in the path of the waves. So a sound that is 80 db at its source might be only 75 db by the time it reaches a listener who is, say, 20 feet away. The amount of reduction in intensity as a sound travels is so dependent on the acoustical environment in which it travels that it is impossible to give a simple formula, but the fact that sound intensity decreases with distance should be kept in mind. Otherwise, you may find what seem to be some astonishingly loud levels when computing output levels of sound systems. One watt of output is, in theory, equivalent to a 120-db intensity level and can, in theory, be reproduced by a 20-watt amplifier with 5 percent efficiency speakers. But theory is not practice, and many conditions contribute to the fact that you cannot actually produce a 120-db level of undistorted sound with a 20-watt amplifier and 5 percent efficiency speakers.

A sound system must perform three functions for theatrical purposes: 1) reinforcement—to amplify actors' voices as they speak or sing on stage; 2) reproduction—to play back prerecorded sound effects or music during a performance; 3) recording—to make show tapes of sound effects and music for playback use during a performance and to record entire concerts or theatrical performances. These functions may be combined in a single overall system or treated separately in two or three systems. For purposes of clarity, I shall discuss them separately.

THE REINFORCEMENT SYSTEM

The basic components of the system are: microphones, mixer/preamplifier, power amplifier, and speakers. In some situations it may be desirable to have an equalizer and/or a reverberation unit within the mixing stage. These might be either separate units or an integral part of a custom-made mixing console. The block diagram in Figure II–1 shows a typical single-channel system. The system could be wired for two channels if desired; this would require either a stereo mixer and stereo amplifier or two separate sets of mono mixers and amplifiers. If the system is to be used solely for reinforcement of small productions, a single channel should be sufficient unless the hall is to be used for musicals, rock concerts, or rock operas, in which case multiple channels are necessary.

Placement of microphones may vary according to the stage plan or the particular production. The layout that is generally considered best for proscenium stages is to have the microphones mounted in acoustical foam on the floor at the front of the stage (Fig. II–2). The main advantage to floor-mounted microphones is that the distance of the reflected signal from the floor is close to the same distance as that of the direct signal from the actor (Fig. II–3). This prevents some phasing problems that would occur if the reflected signal were arriving later than the direct signal. The signals reaching the floor-mounted microphones are fairly simple and direct compared to the complex reflected signal pattern received by a boom-mounted microphone or a suspended microphone, so the resultant sound is cleaner. Floor vibrations and the sound of people walking are reduced to inaudibility by the acoustical foam.

The ideal position for speakers in the reinforcement system is directly over the proscenium arch. Many new theatres have a screened-in space provided for this (Fig. II–4). This position may help to reduce feedback, because the speaker

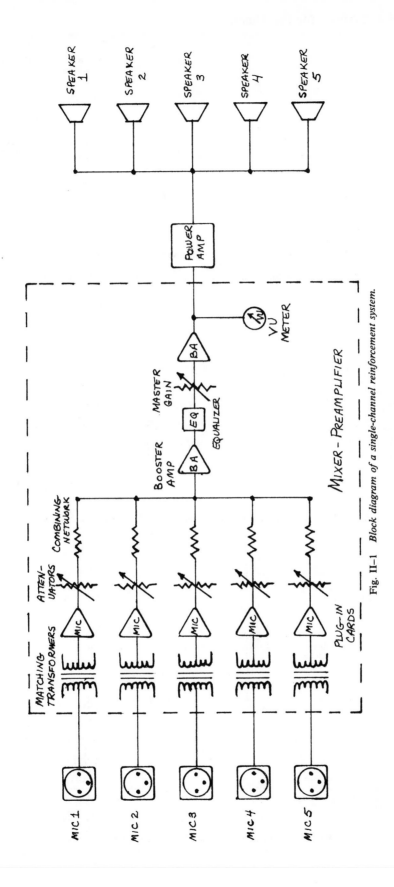

Fig. II-1 *Block diagram of a single-channel reinforcement system.*

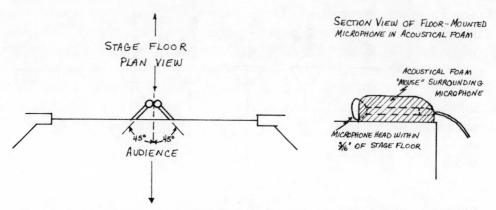

Fig. II–2 *Positions for floor-mounting microphones on proscenium stage and detail of microphone in acoustical foam. Note that two omnidirectional microphones are used head to head at an angle of 45° to the centerline to prevent interference and cancellation effects (discussed in Chapter III).*

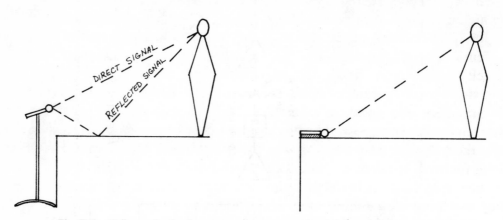

Fig. II–3 *Difference in signal patterns to boom-mounted and floor-mounted microphones.*

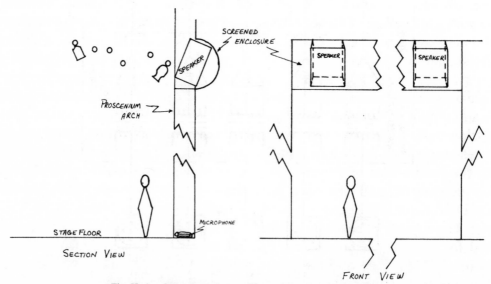

Fig. II–4 *Over-proscenium speaker position for reinforcement.*

signal is in front of the microphones and directed away from them. This position also provides the most realistic directionality to the sound. Human hearing can easily determine direction in a horizontal plane, but not in a vertical one; therefore, the sound coming from a speaker directly above an actor will seem to be coming from the actor.

THE REPRODUCTION SYSTEM

The block diagram in Fig. II–5 shows a typical two-channel reproduction system, which will also accept microphones either for reinforcement or for live mic sound cues. The components are two half-track stereo tape decks, microphones, stereo mixer/preamplifier, stereo power amplifier, and speakers (usually eight or ten for an average-sized theatre). Ideally, there should be a single power amplifier for every speaker, or at least an impedance matching network in the speaker switching or patching panel so that the impedance load on the amplifier outputs never goes below the minimum for safe, efficient operation. In a small theatre with a maximum of four speakers a stereo amplifier would suffice, but the outputs should be tapped off the four-ohm or two-ohm terminals. Again, this system can be made more sophisticated by the addition of an equalizer and a reverberation unit. Although these extras are not essential, they add a new dimension to the possibilities of sound reproduction in theatre, and they are frequently built right into custom mixing consoles. The number of output channels required for a system is determined by the theatre and the type of productions to be done in it. In any case, for current theatrical needs, a single channel is insufficient. Most small and medium-sized theatres with moderate ambitions and budgets can do nicely with a two-channel system, but if the budget will allow, a four-channel system is better because it permits more flexibility.

The system should have enough flexibility to allow for variations of speaker matrixing and movement of sound around the theatre. A proscenium theatre of medium size (seating capacity of 500 to 750) should have at least eight permanent speaker positions: two backstage, two at the proscenium, two midhouse, and two at the rear of the house. (A balcony would necessitate two more at the rear of the balcony level.) There should also be sufficient auxiliary speaker outlets to accommodate small speakers within the stage set for practical cues (radio, television, etc.). An arena theatre would probably need six or eight speakers spaced around the theatre as well as outlets on stage for practical cues. The speaker-switching network at the console should have a four-position switch for each speaker: off, channel A, channel B, and both A & B. (A system of more than two channels would require a different type of switching system to permit the speaker to engage any combination of channels.) Any reproduction system should include a sound motion device. Speakers can be patched into this unit in any sequence, and, by means of a rotary control, the sound will travel smoothly from speaker to speaker in the order in which they are patched.

Flexibility should be considered for the input side of the system as well. Each track of each tape deck should have a separate control; this should include a

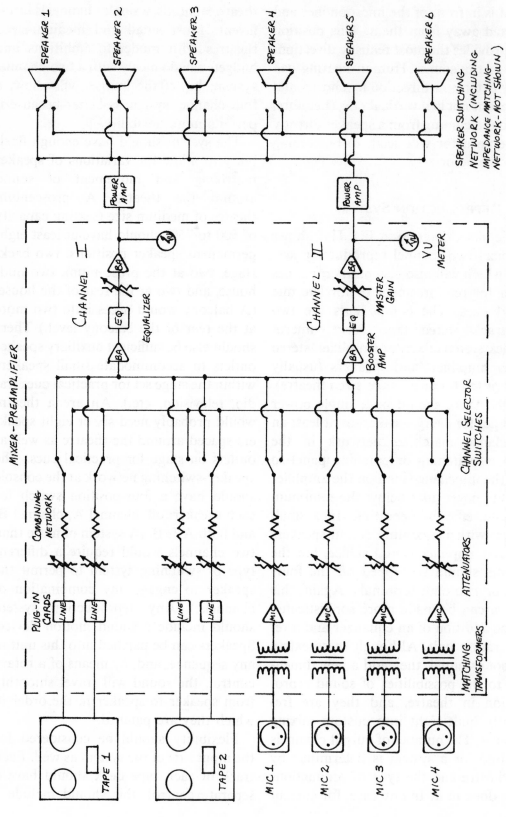

Fig. II-5 Block diagram of two-channel reproduction system.

channel selector switch as well as a volume control, so that any input may be switched to either channel A or channel B or both. (Again, in a four-channel system the switching should permit any combination of output channels.) There should be enough inputs in the system to permit each tape deck to be permanently connected to its own input and still leave sufficient inputs for microphones and auxiliary equipment. For a two-channel/two-deck system, eight inputs is a minimum; for a four-channel system in a large theatre, fourteen or sixteen inputs would be required. In addition to individual inputs there should be a master volume control.

Besides flexibility you must consider ease of operation in your system. Although the system may be able to handle electrically anything you could possibly require it to do, you may find that it is physically impossible for the operator to work enough switches simultaneously to execute the cues. There are ways that you can lay out the system to make operation easier. The mixer should have paired sliders instead of rotating knobs for volume controls, at least for the tape decks. This makes it possible to cross-fade between tape decks even though there are a total of four controls to operate (Fig. II–6). The tape decks should be equipped with some kind of automatic cueing device, so that the operator does not have to worry about stopping and resetting the tapes during fast cue sequences. There are several auto-cue cueing devices on the market; some require an extra head on the deck and the use of

Fig. II–6 *Mixer control panel with sliding attenuator, gain switch, echo send controls, and output selector switches for each input. At right is one of four output master controls with echo return control and meter.*

AUDIO SPECTRUM OF NEW HAVEN

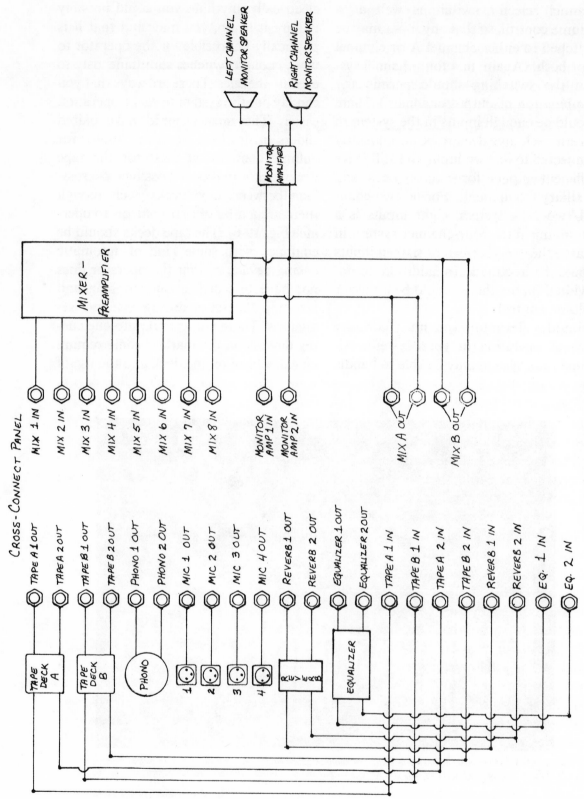

Fig. II-7 *Block diagram of two-channel recording system.*

a special pencil mark or piece of foil on the inside of the tape where you want it to stop. The lead mark or foil strip closes the electrical gap on the special head, which then activates the stop solenoid, stopping the machine within an inch or two. Other devices operate on a photoelectric cell; recording tape and opaque leader tape prevent light from striking the cell, but clear leader tape passes light to the cell, activating the stop solenoid. The tape decks should still be within easy reach of the operator, in case of mechanical failure or tape breakage or a problem on stage causing a cue to be skipped.

The control booth in the theatre should be in a position where the sound operator can see the stage. Many cues are visual, and even though the stage manager is calling the cues, some will be more accurate if the operator can see (for instance, a fade-out timed with an exit). Ideally, the operator should also be able to hear the stage and the sound cues live (as opposed to hearing them over a monitor speaker). That requires a good booth position and a large open window, which, in turn, requires an almost silent functioning of the sound system. A clunky old tape deck would not do in that situation, and even some solenoid machines are too loud when they engage. So it is important to know what kind of a booth the system will be going into before you decide what kind of equipment to buy; if it will be an open booth, make sure the equipment is quiet. The advantages of having an open booth should be obvious. Acoustics will change in any theatre according to the size of the audience. (People absorb sound.) Some sound levels may be critical enough that they will have to be adjusted from night to night depending on whether the house is full or only half-full. In a theatre where shows will require reinforcement, it is essential that the operator be in an open booth. Levels will have to be adjusted according to who is speaking or singing and how distant they are from the microphones. In the event that the reproduction system is in a totally enclosed booth, there should be a speaker attached to the general stage monitor system so that the operator can monitor fades accurately.

When a reinforcement or reproduction system is installed in a theatre, be sure to run all sound cables in separate conduit, and keep them as far away as possible, from lighting cables, electrical winch cables, or anything else that might cause noise in the system. You may think you can save money by installing the system yourself, but if you do it incorrectly you may have wasted the cost of the system: unless you use shielded cable of the proper size, run properly in conduit, your expensive new equipment will go buzz, hum, crackle, sputter, and may even pick up the local radio station.

THE RECORDING SYSTEM

The block diagram in Figure II–7 shows a typical two-channel recording system. The basic components are a variable-speed turntable, two half-track stereo tape decks, microphones, stereo mixer/preamplifier, stereo power amplifier, monitor speakers, and cross-connect panel. The cross-connect panel is essential for allowing flexibility (Fig. II–8). The output of any component can be connected to the input of any other com-

Fig. II–8 *Typical recording system cross-connect panel.*

ponent, and auxiliary components can be added at any time. Other components that you could expect to see in a well-equipped recording studio are: reverberation unit, graphic equalizer, signal generators, such as sine/square wave or white noise generators. If there is money in the budget, an electronic synthesizer would be a nice addition to any studio. A studio that will be used to make complex sound cues and multiple mixes should have either at least three half-track tape decks or one four-track (four-channel) and two half-track tape decks. The decks should have remote-control operation from the console so that two or three decks can be started simultaneously. Needless to say, there is nothing wrong with having more than two output channels; the more

channels you have, the more flexible your system can be. Several companies now offer modular recording consoles that can be expanded as your budget permits: begin with twelve inputs and two outputs in your mixer; then the next year increase it to four outputs; a few years later expand to twenty inputs and eight outputs. This kind of flexibility is very desirable.

Other important considerations when setting up a recording system are ease in handling and maximum efficiency in the function of each component. Tape decks should be mounted at the optimum angle for easy threading and accurate reading of controls. They should be mounted with enough space for 10½-inch reels, which might overhang the sides, to clear any nearby equipment. One deck should be mounted horizontally, or close to it, with some counter space in front and to the sides for easy editing. The turntable should be mounted separately from any other equipment to isolate it from bumps and vibrations. Auxiliary equipment should be rack-mounted and easily accessible. These points may seem obvious, but a poorly designed studio will not only waste time but will usually contribute to early breakdown of equipment.

If the studio is to be used for much live recording, it would be wise to have separate recording and control rooms. The control room should be large enough to handle all the equipment and operators comfortably, leaving some room for expansion. The recording room should be large enough to handle all types of recording that might need to be done. If the budget can afford it, there should be adjustable acoustical panels so that the ambience (reverberation characteristics) of the recording space can be changed. If this is not possible, then make the space fairly dead; reverberation can always be added to a dead recording, but it cannot be removed if there is too much to start with. One caution: do not use fluorescent light fixtures in a recording studio—they will add a 60-cycle hum to your live recordings.

If the recording system is separate from the reproduction system, there should be a similarity of equipment, particularly speakers, between the two systems. While you are creating sound cues it is important to listen to them in an acoustical situation similar to that in which they will be played back for performance. Speakers tend to add more of their own tone coloration to sound and music than any other piece of equipment. For this reason the monitor speakers in the recording studio should match the reproduction speakers in the theatre.

MATCHING COMPONENTS WITHIN A SYSTEM

Several situations arise in which you might be asked to specify a sound system or portions thereof. If you are lucky, the theatre will allocate enough money to purchase an entire system all at once. If there is not enough money for that, the theatre may allocate a small amount for "improving the existing system." This is sometimes difficult and often a waste of money: a system can sound only as good as its lowest-quality component. You might, of course, be in the situation where one component of your existing system is of considerably lower quality than the rest, and if you replace this component with one that matches the quality of the rest of the system you will indeed

be making an improvement. But most of the time you will end up improving one component above the quality of the others, and this will often make the system sound worse than it did before (by revealing faults in the other components that had previously been inaudible). Most of my remarks in this section, therefore, refer to the case where you are called upon to specify an entire new system, thus putting you in a position to match the components to each other carefully.

The first consideration is frequency response and range. Overall you want a flat frequency response, one with little deviation. That is, there should be little or no difference in reproduction of a 400-Hz tone and a 5000-Hz tone (Fig. II–9a). If a system does not have a flat frequency response, it is said to "color" the sound. For example, Figure II–9b shows a system with a peak at around 100 Hz; this system would sound boomy. Another system that had a peak at 5000 Hz and had little or no bass response would sound tinny. When a composer creates sound effects or music, he wants to be able to make his own tone colorations

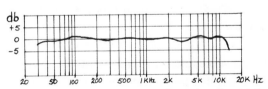

Fig. II–9a *Freqncy response curve of typical system with flat response.*

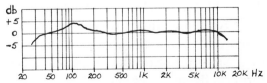

Fig. II–9b *Frequency response curve of system with peak at 100 Hz.*

and not be stuck with unwanted colorations from the sound system.

The overall frequency range of a system depends on the theatre and its uses (to be discussed in the next section). It is important, however, to match the frequency range of components within a system; in general, the frequency range of the output components should not be significantly greater than that of the input components. If it is, the system will be reproducing a lot of unnecessary noise. Let us say, for example, that the tape deck reproduces within a range of 50 to 8000 Hz and that the amplifiers and speakers reproduce accurately from 20 to 20,000 Hz. This means that although you are not reproducing any sound effects from 20 to 50 Hz and from 8K to 20K Hz, you are reproducing hiss and system hum. If your speakers reproduced only up to 8K Hz, then you would still be getting the same amount of sound effects and considerably less noise. If, on the other hand, you have a very fine tape deck that reproduces from 30 to 18K Hz, and assuming your recording system is good enough to make tapes of that frequency range, but your speakers only reproduce from 50 to 8000 Hz, then you are missing a great deal of the color and quality of your sound effects. It would seem senseless to have spent the money on a high-quality recording system if the sounds will not be reproduced in the theatre, when for a few dollars more the system could have been matched so that it would reproduce your sounds fully.

There can be much misunderstanding when discussing power in a sound system. Simply stating the amplifier power rating tells you nothing unless you also know the efficiency of your speakers—what percentage of electrical power from the amplifier is actually translated into physical sound power. A 1 percent efficient speaker will produce a sound-pressure level that is (in watts per square meter) $\frac{1}{100}$ of the output of the amplifier. It will take 100 watts of amplifier power to produce a sound-pressure level of 1w/m². This should not worry you in any way; 1w/m² is the equivalent of 120 decibels (db) of sound power, which is the threshold of pain. For most theatrical purposes you should not need to produce more than 115 db, but some sounds will need to be that loud to have the effect you want. In order to achieve that volume without distortion, a 1 percent efficient speaker will need to be driven by a 40- to 50-watt amplifier; a 0.5 percent efficient speaker will need to be driven by 80 to 100 watts to produce 115 db. Because of the types of sounds and the loud volumes to which theatrical speakers are subjected, they must be unusually durable. Most music is not played at continuously high volumes; only the loudest sections hit 110 or 115 db. Also, most music (with the exception of electronic music) does not contain continuous high-frequency signals of significant amplitude. Quite often, however, the sound effects for a theatrical production do contain high-frequency signals of long duration and high volume. This can burn out a tweeter or at least blow its protective fuse. Woofers are not immune to destruction either. Loud, low frequency signals, particularly pure sine waves, are not kind to speakers. So make sure the speakers you choose can withstand the power peaks of your amplifier. (An amplifier with a continuous power rating of 80 watts may hit more than twice that wattage on instantaneous power peaks.)

A frequent problem in older systems, and one which should still be considered when putting together a new system, is impedance mismatching. A general rule of thumb is that the input impedance should be ten times the source or output impedance, to simplify operation. Input impedances of mixers and power amplifiers should be at least 10,000 ohms. A mixer with low impedance inputs (say 600 ohms) may work well enough with a tape deck (standard output impedance of 600 ohms), but it will lose gain and possibly distort when it meets the output of an older tube-type mixer with an impedance of several thousand ohms. This situation might also occur in a recording studio that still has some older model filters and signal generators in use. These tube models usually have much higher output impedances—as high as 10,000 ohms. Tape deck input impedances should be noted. Although most are 10,000 ohms or more, some still run as low as 600 ohms. In this case certain equipment with high output impedances cannot be plugged directly into the tape deck inputs, but must go through the mixer (assuming that the mixer output should be 600 ohms). Knowledge of impedance matching is particularly important in systems that use an open patch panel—where you can easily connect from any output to any input.

TRACING THROUGH A SYSTEM AND TROUBLESHOOTING

There is a logic to sound systems, and once you understand this logic you should be able to operate any sound system and to pinpoint trouble spots when a system is not working properly. Although the interior design and engineering may differ, and you needn't know the details of that engineering; all systems are based on the same principles. There are four basic stages in sound systems: the input or sound source; preamplification and mixing; amplification; and output. The precise equipment comprising each stage will vary according to the functions of the system and the sophistication of its design, but you should be able to recognize where a piece of equipment belongs in a system, and if a system does not work you should be able to find which component or which connection is causing the trouble. The sound-source stage will consist of a microphone, a tape deck, a turntable, or a signal generator (in the broad sense, anything that generates a sound signal). The second stage will contain some sort of preamplifier and mixer; this may or may not contain filters, echo units, and other sound-altering devices. In systems used strictly for reinforcement or reproduction (Fig. II–1), the outputs of the mixer are usually connected directly to the amplification stage, which in turn is connected to the speakers. A speaker switching network will be either between the mixer and the amplifiers, or between the amplifiers and the speakers, depending on whether there is a power amplifier only for each output channel or one for every speaker. (The latter is now the preferred method and has recently become financially as feasible as the former method.) Systems that are used for recording (Fig. II–7) will usually have a patch panel, and the outputs of the mixer will go both to the patch panel and to a power amplifier that drives the monitor speakers. The outputs of the mixer can then be fed into the inputs of a tape deck for recording. (The tape deck outputs may then be fed either directly to the monitor amplifier or through the mixer to the amplifier and monitor speakers. If the latter is the case, make sure the two signals [that going into the tape deck and that coming out] are on two separate channels of the mixer. Otherwise you create a closed feedback loop that will send the system into self-oscillation.)

If a system is not functioning properly, the first thing is to isolate the trouble. Often it is a simple problem that any operator can fix, and there is no need to call a repairman. To isolate the trouble spot, simply trace back through the system. Most mixers and most tape decks are equipped with VU meters, which make the process easier. For example, if the system is patched so that sound should be coming from the monitor speakers but is not, check the meters on the mixer. If those meters are reading but there is no sound, then the problem must be between the mixer and the speaker (probably a loose or shorted speaker connection). If the meters on the mixer are not reading, then the problem is either at the mixer (a volume control is down which should be up) or before the mixer. If the sound source is the tape deck, check its meters; if they are reading, then the problem may be in the patch panel (a shorted plug). If the sound source is the turntable or other sound generator with no meter, patch it directly to the tape deck and see if you get a reading on the record meters. If you do, the problem is at the mixer; if you don't, the problem is in the patch panel

or in the sound source. This process becomes instinctive after a while, particularly if you work with the same system for any length of time. The principles you learn on one system can be applied to any system; even if the equipment is entirely different, the principles remain the same.

MATCHING A SYSTEM TO THE NEEDS OF A SPECIFIC THEATRE

In the past decade many companies have sprung up throughout the United States that build "custom" sound systems for any type of installation. Most of these companies are quite reputable and can indeed give you a system that will do just about anything you could want it to do in the field of sound. The catch is that you must know what you want a system to be able to do for you and what you will sacrifice to get a system to fit within your budget. Many of these companies have consultants who are well versed in the needs of commercial recording studios (which make records and demo tapes of rock groups, record the local high-school glee club, etc.), but very few consultants really know the sound requirements of a legitimate theatre. There are five questions you must be able to answer before you go shopping for a sound system.

First, what type of system do you want; what is its function? Do you need just a reproduction system? Will you want two systems, one for reinforcement and reproduction in the theatre and one for recording in a separate studio? Perhaps you already have an adequate reproduction system which has doubled, inadequately, as a recording studio. You may wish to purchase a new recording system and merely upgrade the existing reproduction system. The type of system you need will determine not only what equipment it will contain, but also how complex the mixing console will be. It is primarily in the mixing console that you get a custom-made system.

Second, the size of the theatre should be considered, particularly if it is a reinforcement or reproduction system you are buying. The size of the theatre will determine first of all whether or not you need reinforcement. The size of the stage will determine how many microphone inputs are needed. The size of both the stage and the house will determine how many speakers are needed, and this in turn may have some effect on how many output channels you decide to have. If you have a very small theatre with only a few speaker positions, it may be less expensive with little drop in quality to have a single power amplifier for each output channel, whereas in a large theatre with ten or twelve speakers you will surely need an individual amplifier for every speaker.

Third, what type of productions will be done in your theatre? If you intend to do large-scale musicals you will need a reinforcement system. If that is all you intend to do, you may need only one playback deck for the occasional sound effects called for in musical comedies. If you will be doing dramatic works as well, then you should have two tape decks and at least two output channels. Probably the more experimental the nature of your productions, the more flexible and sophisticated your sound systems will need to be. If you always do very conventional productions you can get by with much less. You should also consider whether

the theatre will be used for other functions besides play production. If concerts are frequently given, you may want your system to be able to record them as well as reproducing sound effects for theatrical productions. You may want provisions for connecting the sound output of a movie projector through the system if the hall is frequently used for showing films.

Fourth, of course, your system will largely be determined by how much money you have to spend on it. If possible, you should write up detailed specifications for the system and put it up for bid to several different companies. If you do this, however, be sure to include installation, service, and maintenance in your specifications. You may be able to reduce costs by supplying semiskilled labor for the installation so that the company has to send only one supervisor on the installation trip. The budget for sound systems should be proportional to the total technical budget of the theatre. The quality of your sound effects should be at least equivalent to the quality of the scenery, costumes, and lights. If your specifications far exceed your budget you will have to sacrifice; the choice is usually among quantity, quality, and flexibility. By cutting back on the expenditure per speaker and amplifier you may be able to retain flexibility at the console and lose only in the area of total sound power output. Only you can decide what features are most necessary for your theatre. In the case of a recording system you may be able to get a modular system, buying only the bare minimum one year and expanding it a little each year.

The final question to be considered in planning new sound systems is who will operate and maintain the systems. If you are in a school where most of the running crew positions are filled by acting and directing students who are not in that particular production, then a flexible, sophisticated system may exceed their operating capabilities. On the other hand, if you have sufficient technical personnel and are in the business of training technicians, you should have a system that is a challenge to them and that will constantly push them to expand their creative facilities. You should also consider how often the equipment will change hands and whether it will be subject to possible mishandling by unskilled beginners. In general, the more flexible and sophisticated a system is, the more delicate it is. What they say about automobiles holds true for sound equipment: "They don't build 'em like they used to." It is rumored in the business that certain old tape decks could be dropped off the back of a truck and still come up working. Of course these old machines didn't have solenoid controls, echo and sound-on-sound functions, and other deluxe features found on current machines. But it may be that for the people who will be operating the equipment, you should have a less sophisticated, more durable model. When you do purchase a system, make sure there is a service and maintenance clause in the contract. If the company is not within easy driving distance from your theatre, make sure there is someone in your area who can handle emergency maintenance (either an electronics technician at the theatre or a local hi-fi store with a good repair shop). It could be very discouraging to have one small burned-out transistor prevent you from having any sound for three weeks because you had to ship the component half-way across the country. You may wish to purchase a slightly less sophisticated system from a local company than to get a complex, but not easily maintained, system from a distant company.

In this chapter I shall discuss the use and care of equipment. I wish to avoid naming specific brands, and where a name does appear it is not an endorsement or recommendation but an illustration of some facet of the equipment. There are many good brands of equipment on the market. (Most companies dealing in *professional* sound equipment are equally reputable.) Each brand has its own set of special features. What is right for your system depends on your theatre and its financial status, not on my personal taste. This chapter is written in a somewhat general fashion to allow for the technical advances that will take place over the next few years. A piece of equipment that is the best money can buy at this writing may be obsolete by the time this book is published.

THE TAPE DECK

A *tape deck* (Fig. III–1), technically, is a machine that will record an electrical signal onto magnetic tape that passes across the record head at a designated speed, and reproduce that signal when the tape passes across the playback head at the same speed. The section of the deck that contains the reel motors, head assembly, and capstan drive is called the *tape transport*. The section that contains the function switches, record preamplifi-ers, level controls, meters, and other electrical features is called the electronics. If a machine also contains its own amplifier and speaker it is technically called a *tape recorder*. (A tape deck must be connected to a separate amplifier and speaker.) A *tape reproducer* is the tape transport without the electronics and without a record head; the playback head is connected directly to a preamplifier, and the machine can be used to play back prerecorded tapes.

A tape deck has five operational modes: *play, rewind, fast forward, record,* and *edit*. (The edit mode is optional; it is not found on every tape deck.) The play mode permits playback of prerecorded tapes. The tape is held against the head assembly as it moves from the left *feed* reel to the right *take-up* reel. Only the playback head functions in this mode. The rewind mode moves the tape at a rapid speed from right to left, back onto the feed reel. Usually the tape is held away from the heads in this mode, although some machines are equipped with a tape-lift defeat mechanism that allows the tape to pass across the heads. Since the playback head does function in this mode, it is possible to locate beginnings and ends of recorded passages very rapidly by means of the tape-lift defeat mechanism. The fast-forward mode functions in the same manner as rewind

1. FEED REEL
2. TAKE-UP REEL
3. TAPE COUNTER
4. TAPE GUIDE w/ SMALL TENSION ARM
5. HEAD BLOCK ASSEMBLY
6. PINCH ROLLER
7. CAPSTAN
8. TENSION ARM
9. POWER ON-OFF SWITCH
10. SPEED SELECTION SWITCH
11. REEL SIZE SELECTION SWITCH
12. TAPE LIFT DEFEAT MECHANISM
13. RECORD BUTTON
14. REWIND BUTTON
15. STOP BUTTON
16. PLAY BUTTON
17. FAST FORWARD BUTTON
18. PLAY BACK VOLUME CONTROL
19. RECORD-SAFETY SWITCH
20. MIC INPUT VOLUME CONTROL
21. LINE INPUT VOLUME CONTROL
22. VU METER
23. MONITOR SELECTION SWITCH
24. PEAK-READING LED

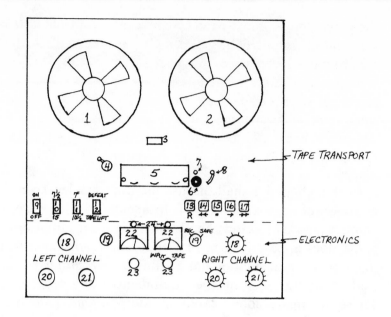

Fig. III–1   *Typical two-channel tape deck.*

but in the opposite direction, moving from left to right onto the take-up reel. To engage a machine in the record mode usually requires pushing both a special record button and the play button; it may also require switching the electronics from a safety condition to a ready record condition. The reason for this is that in the record mode both the record and erase heads function. Anything that was previously recorded on a tape will be erased when the machine is engaged in the record mode. The safety device is to prevent the accidental erasure of recorded tapes. When in the record mode the playback head also functions, and it is possible to monitor from the playback head (listen to the signal that has just been recorded). It is also possible to monitor the original input signal, before it has been recorded. The electronics will usually contain a switch labeled something like SOURCE—TAPE or IN-PUT—REPRODUCE, which enables the operator to select which signal he will monitor. By means of this switch it is possible to make a direct A-B comparison between the source signal and the recorded signal to determine whether any audible noise or distortion is being added during the recording process. The edit mode will vary from machine to machine, but its purpose is to enable the editor to move the tape across the playback head manually, at a very slow speed, and hear the signal. The functioning of this mode usually involves a tape-lift defeat mechanism, which may be combined with a disengagement of the reel motors to permit free tape movement backward and forward.

On all current professional tape decks,

the play, stop, and fast-wind controls are solenoid-operated. (The solenoid is an electromagnetic device for actuating switches and relays.) The advantages of electrical over mechanical controls are numerous. The machine has a much smoother start and can attain correct speed much more rapidly. The electrical controls permit the operator to go directly back and forth between the rewind and fast forward modes without damage to the equipment or the tape. This makes rapid cueing much easier and more accurate. Logic circuits may be introduced into electrical controls to prevent damage to equipment or tapes no matter in what order or how rapidly the controls are pushed. In other words, while the machine is in fast forward the operator can push the play button and the machine will first come to a complete stop and then engage in the play mode. This type of machine, with built-in logic circuits, is ideal for any installation that is likely to be in the hands of beginners. Solenoid controls permit the use of an electronic cueing device. This would take the form of an extra head, light sensor, or other sensing device which, upon sensing the correct signal from the tape, will close a circuit and activate the stop solenoid, stopping the machine at a specifically cued point in the tape. Solenoid controls also permit the use of remote-control switches so that the tape decks can be operated from a control console. A certain amount of care should be taken to keep dirt away from the controls. If the contacts become dirty the solenoids may not engage properly. Any electronics technician will be able to clean them, but if the machine is still under warranty this should be done by an authorized serviceman. In any case try to avoid such typical theatre grime as sawdust, cigarette ashes, coffee, and soft drinks.

Any current professional tape deck has at least three heads (Fig. III–2). They are always, in order from left to right, the *erase head,* the *record head,* and the *playback head.* Some machines have one or more extra heads. To the left of the erase head is any sensing head for an automatic cueing device. To the right of the playback head are any extra playback heads, for instance, a quarter-track playback head on a half-track machine. All heads should be cleaned after approximately ten hours of use. Use clean Q-tips and alcohol to clean the heads and any other parts with which the tape comes in contact (tape guides, capstan, pinch roller). The heads should be degaussed or demagnetized approximately once every twenty hours of use. This can be done with any commercial head degausser, fol-

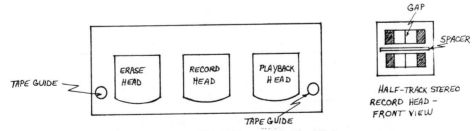

Fig. III–2 *Headblock assembly (simplified).*
[small drawing at right] *Half-track stereo record head—front view.*

lowing the instructions that come with it. Most important is to make sure that the tape deck is off and that there are no tapes within five or ten feet when you use the degausser.

The standard speeds for recording tapes are 3¾ inches per second (ips), 7½ ips, 15 ips, and 30 ips. The faster the tape speed, the greater the fidelity of the recording, and the easier the tape is to edit. Master tapes for commercial classical records are usually made at 30 ips. For purposes of theatrical sound effects 7½ ips is fairly standard, and the fidelity of current equipment at that speed is very good, although some sound designers prefer to use 15 ips for making master tapes of original sound effects. The 3¾-ips speed is not really good enough for theatrical work, although it is handy to have for dubbing sounds at half speed to create certain effects. Most machines have two speeds, some have three. If you have two two-speed machines, it is useful to have one 7½ and 15 and the other 3¾ and 7½. This provides greater flexibility and enables you to play almost any prerecorded tape. Each speed on the professional tape deck has its own equalization adjustment. Equalization is the adjustment of frequency response to compensate for inherent frequency response characteristics of the tape and the heads at a given speed (Fig. III–3). It also pro-

vides a uniform current to the record head. This adjustment may be made automatically through the same switching system as the tape speed, or it may be a separate switch. If your deck does not have a separate switch labeled EQUALIZATION, then it is done automatically when you choose the tape speed. There is also a switch, probably labeled REEL SIZE or the equivalent, which will adjust the tape tension correctly for either 7-inch or 10½-inch reels. Most professional machines do not have a tension adjustment for reel sizes smaller than 7 inches; 5-inch and 3-inch reels may be used, but you should do so with caution, as the tension will be tighter than it should be.

Several different *tracking* configurations are available in professional and semiprofessional tape decks (Fig. III–4). Outdated but still around is the full-track, monaural head; its uses are limited and it should, when possible, be replaced by a multitrack model. Most common in theatrical use is the half-track, stereo head. For use with ¼-inch-wide tape, this configuration gives the best fidelity with some flexibility. The narrower the width of the recorded track, the lower the fidelity of the recording and the greater the crosstalk between tracks. Some semiprofessional tape decks have a four-track quadraphonic head configuration for ¼-

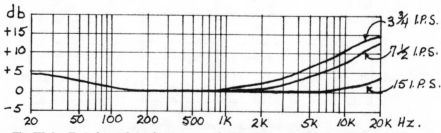

Fig. III–3 *Typical record equalization curves for ¼-inch tape decks using NAB characteristics.*

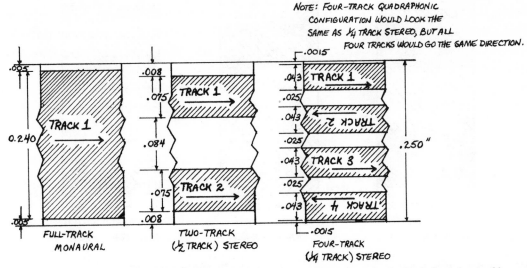

Fig. III–4 *Quarter-inch tape tracking configurations. Note: Four-track quadraphonic configuration would look the same as ¼-track stereo, but all four tracks would go the same direction.*

inch tape with decent fidelity, and these machines are useful when doing complex mixes; but if possible a ½-inch tape width should be used for four-track machines. The quarter-track stereo configuration is not very useful for theatre systems; the fidelity is not as good as half-track stereo, and it is undesirable to record in two directions on one tape because of the difficulty in editing. There is some compatibility among tracking configurations, but there will always be some signal loss and added noise when a tape is played on different type heads (Fig. III–5). For instance, a tape that was recorded on a full-track monaural machine can be played back on a half-track stereo machine; the original sound will be heard, but there will be some signal loss in the center of the tape where there is no gap in the half-track head, and there will be some additional noise from the edges of the tape where the unrecorded portions of the tape pass across the gaps of the half-track head. Complete incom-patibility occurs when a tape that has been recorded in both directions (say a quarter-track stereo tape recorded "both sides") is played on either a full-track or a half-track stereo machine; all the sound on the tape will be heard—half of it correctly and half of it backwards.

One of the most difficult recording concepts to understand is the *bias current*. The bias current is applied to the tape through the record head during the recording process; it is a very high frequency current, usually three to five times the highest frequency to be recorded—or between 50,000 and 250,000 Hz. It is completely independent of the audio signal and in no way modulates with it; the wavelength is so small that it is not "read" by the playback head and therefore is not reproduced in playback. The purpose of applying a bias current is to reduce the distortion created by the nonlinear characteristics of magnetic-oxide tape (Fig. III–6). Although the oxide characteristic curve is nonlinear

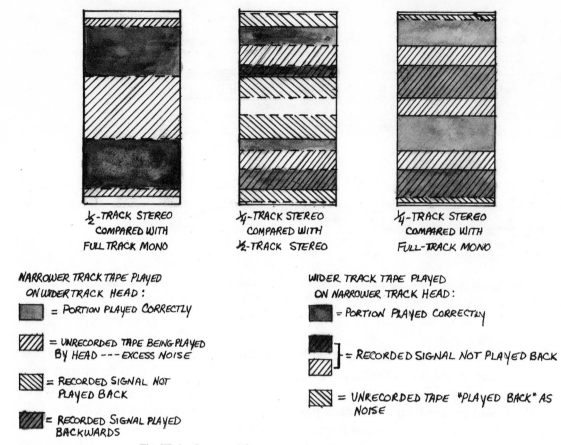

½-TRACK STEREO COMPARED WITH FULL TRACK MONO

¼-TRACK STEREO COMPARED WITH ½-TRACK STEREO

¼-TRACK STEREO COMPARED WITH FULL-TRACK MONO

NARROWER TRACK TAPE PLAYED ON WIDER TRACK HEAD:

■ = PORTION PLAYED CORRECTLY

▨ = UNRECORDED TAPE BEING PLAYED BY HEAD --- EXCESS NOISE

▨ = RECORDED SIGNAL NOT PLAYED BACK

▨ = RECORDED SIGNAL PLAYED BACKWARDS

WIDER TRACK TAPE PLAYED ON NARROWER TRACK HEAD:

■ = PORTION PLAYED CORRECTLY

■
▨ } = RECORDED SIGNAL NOT PLAYED BACK

▨ = UNRECORDED TAPE "PLAYED BACK" AS NOISE

Fig. III-5   *Incompatibility among different tracking configurations.*

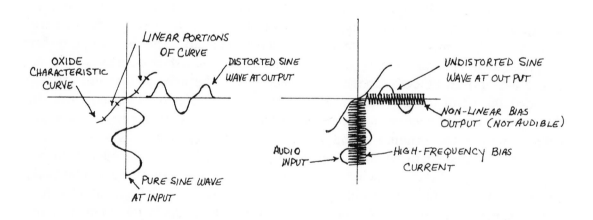

OXIDE CHARACTERISTIC CURVE

LINEAR PORTIONS OF CURVE

DISTORTED SINE WAVE AT OUTPUT

PURE SINE WAVE AT INPUT

NO BIAS CURRENT APPLIED

UNDISTORTED SINE WAVE AT OUTPUT

NON-LINEAR BIAS OUTPUT (NOT AUDIBLE)

AUDIO INPUT

HIGH-FREQUENCY BIAS CURRENT

BIAS CURRENT APPLIED AT INPUT.

Fig. III-6   *Characteristics of magnetic oxide tape and the effects of bias current.*

when viewed overall, certain portions of it are linear. The bias current places the audio signal onto the linear portion of that curve and effectively reduces the distortion. Unfortunately, the bias current affects more than just the distortion; it also has a pronounced effect on frequency response, sensitivity, and signal-to-noise ratio. These, of course, are not coordinated—the optimum bias for low distortion is not the same as the optimum bias for good frequency response. In fact, the optimum bias varies for different frequencies. This means there must be a compromise among all these dependent characteristics to find the one bias adjustment that gives the best overall response. Again, unfortunately, this compromise bias adjustment varies among tape types. Regular iron-oxide tapes require a lower bias level than the chromium-dioxide tapes, and even among iron-oxide tapes there are differences in optimum bias settings dependent on particle shape and chemical treatment. Many tape decks come with a bias switch enabling you to preset two bias settings—usually one for regular tape and one for low noise–high output tape. If possible, you should decide in advance what one or two types of tape you will use consistently in your recording studio. Then have your serviceman adjust the bias to the optimum level for that particular tape (or two tapes if you have a switch). The bias does not affect the playback of prerecorded tapes; it is functional only in the record mode.

THE TURNTABLE

When choosing a turntable for a theatre recording studio, the first quality you should consider is ruggedness or durability. Many different people will use the machine, some of them amateurs who will unknowingly mishandle it. The more expensive home stereo turntables are delicate pieces of equipment, and although they have many refinements and deluxe features, they will not withstand the punishment of a typical theatre recording studio. There are several professional machines that offer some added features while still retaining durability. It is advisable to get a manual, single-play turntable as opposed to an automatic record changer. You will have no need for the multiple-play facility in the studio, and these machines are not as precise or as rugged as manual models. Check the drive mechanism of any turntable you are considering: a belt drive (as opposed to idler wheel drive) will reduce rumble and flutter and is less accident-prone. (If power is cut off from an idler drive turntable while the idler wheel is still engaged, the idler wheel will remain pressed against the platter base, creating a flat spot on the idler wheel. This will cause uneven platter rotation in the future. No damage can be done to a belt drive turntable through accidental power cutoff.) Two extra features that are very useful in studio work are a damped tone arm cueing mechanism and a continuously variable speed control. If you cannot get a variable speed control, at least get a machine with three speeds— $33\frac{1}{3}$, 45, and 78 rpm.

Once you have a sturdy turntable, preferably belt-driven, with a heavy platter, the only other items of concern are the tone arm and cartridge. The cartridge you choose should, of course, be stereo and should suit the needs of your studio. If the majority of the records to be played are sound-effects records, you will not need a very fine, high-priced cartridge; in fact, you would probably be better off with an inexpensive model with a limited frequency range, which will not reproduce as much of the surface noise on these records. If, on the other hand, you will be playing mostly high-quality music records, then by all means get a more expensive cartridge. The advantages in a more expensive cartridge are greater tracking ability at a lower tracking force, smoother frequency response, and extended frequency range. It is this last "advantage" that can sometimes make an expensive cartridge sound worse than an inexpensive one. The broader frequency range exposes background and surface noises that were previously inaudible, while at the same time it cannot enhance any audio signal which is itself limited in frequency range. No matter what type of records you play and what model cartridge you have, you should check the stylus frequently and replace it at the first sign of wear. (You should change the stylus at least once a year, and more frequently if the turntable gets a great deal of use.) The stylus should be cleaned frequently, using a camel-hair brush and alcohol: stroke the alcohol-dampened brush along the stylus *from back to front only.* (When cleaning is being done, make sure the amplifier is off or the volume turned down, so the sound of the brush across the stylus will not reach the speakers.)

You should use the cartridge manufacturer's recommendations as to proper tracking force. Balancing the tone arm and setting the correct tracking force is done in the following manner: with the cartridge and stylus in position, "zero balance" the arm by moving the counterweight at the rear of the arm until the arm is balanced level in midair. Most tone arms have a method of dialing the correct amount of stylus force once the arm is zero balanced. If your tone arm does not have such a calibrated dial, or if you don't trust the calibrations, use an external stylus gauge to adjust the counterweight or the dial to give the proper stylus force (Fig. III–7). Many current turntable models include an antiskating force adjustment. "Skating," the tendency for the tone arm to move toward the center of the record, is caused by friction that is present with angled tone arms. (Tone arms are angled at the cartridge end to improve the tracking angle. With a straight arm the tracking angle is cor-

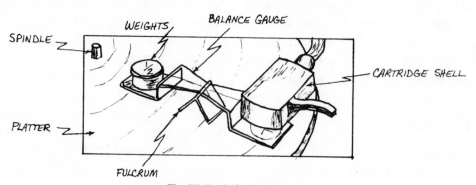

Fig. III–7 *Stylus force gauge.*

rect—that is, with the stylus tangent to the record groove—at only one point on the record, and the error in tracking angle increases rapidly on either side of that correct point. With an angled tone arm the tracking angle is correct at two points and there is almost negligible error throughout the rest of the record.) The antiskating device provides an outward pull, equal and opposite to the skating force. The effect of skating is to increase stylus force on the inner wall of the groove (as the tone arm is forced toward the center) and decrease the force on the outer wall. This may mean there is insufficient tracking force on the outer wall, and distortion will occur. If there is no antiskating adjustment, this distortion can be somewhat compensated for by increasing the stylus force. When there is an antiskating device, adjustment can be made by following the guide in the turntable manual according to the size and shape of the stylus and the desired tracking force, or by playing a heavily recorded passage that is sure to mistrack and adjusting the antiskating until the distortion is equal in both channels.

MICROPHONES

The three types of microphones most common in theatre work are the *dynamic* or moving-coil microphone, the *ribbon* microphone, and the *condenser* microphone. The function of any microphone is to transfer acoustical energy into electrical energy. The dynamic microphone consists of a diaphragm attached to a voice coil, which moves within a permanent magnetic field. The diaphragm responds to the pressure of sound waves striking it and moves the voice coil corre-

spondingly. The coil moving within the magnetic field produces a voltage according to the amount of pressure at the diaphragm. The dynamic microphone is known as a pressure type microphone.

The ribbon microphone is known as a velocity or pressure-gradient type microphone. It consists of a very thin corrugated aluminum foil ribbon suspended within a strong magnetic field. The ribbon is open to sound pressure from both sides and vibrates according to the difference in pressure from the two sides. When the ribbon moves within the magnetic field it produces a voltage corresponding to the particle velocity of the sound pressure wave.

The condenser or capacitor microphone is also a pressure type microphone. The condenser microphone head consists of a two-plate capacitor, one plate being a diaphragm and the other a back plate. When a sound pressure wave strikes the diaphragm, the movement of the diaphragm causes a change in the space between the two capacitor plates, thus causing a change in capacitance. This voltage is amplified and sent through an output transformer. The major disadvantage of the condenser microphone, until a few years ago, was its size. The front plate (diaphragm) of the capacitor must have a constant charge, so it was necessary to have a power supply in the microphone. Also, because the impedance of the capacitor head is extremely high, the microphone must contain its own preamplifier within a few inches of the capacitor head. These preamplification circuits used to be bulky and also required a power supply. Now, however, with the advent of the electret principle and the use of tiny field-effect

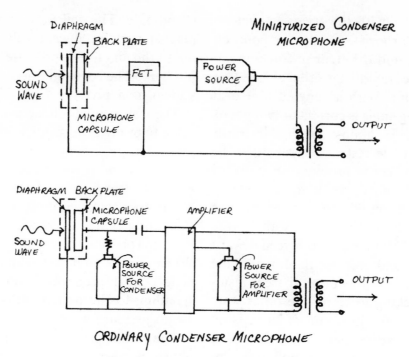

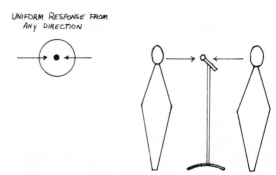

Fig. III–8 *Condenser microphone circuits.*

transistor (FET) circuits for amplification, the condenser microphone can even be miniaturized (Fig. III–8). It was discovered that certain materials will hold an electrostatic charge long after they have been exposed to a strong electric field. This is the electret principle. A high-polymer plastic film is imprinted with an electrostatic charge and used as the diaphragm of the capacitor. This eliminates the need for a power supply for the capacitor. The field-effect transistor is a voltage-controlled device that functions similarly to a vacuum tube. It has an extremely high input impedance and requires only a small source of power, such as 1.5 V battery. The FET is itself quite small, making it possible to build self-contained condenser microphones as small as dynamic microphones and even smaller.

One of the major functional differences among microphones is the direc-

tionality or polar response. An *omnidirectional* microphone responds equally well to sound coming at it from any direction (Fig. III–9). An omni-directional microphone is of a dynamic or condenser type. A *bi-directional* microphone responds to sounds striking it on axis from either side, but the response tapers off to nothing at the ends (Fig. III–10). A bi-directional microphone is usually a ribbon type, although certain double-

Fig. III–9 *Polar response pattern of an omnidirectional microphone.*

headed dynamic and condenser microphones are bi-directional. A *directional* or *cardioid* microphone responds to sounds striking it on axis and rejects sounds from 180° off axis (Fig. III–11). The pattern of rejection varies according to microphone design. Also, because of the shorter wavelength, higher frequencies are rejected more than low frequencies, so most polar-response diagrams indicate curves for four or five frequencies. The rejection of off-axis sound is usually accomplished by means of sound cancellation. The microphone case contains rear-entry ports with delay mechanisms, so that sound entering through the rear-entry port arrives at the rear of the diaphragm at the same time that the same sound arrives at the front of the diaphragm through the microphone head (Fig. III–12). Identical waves traveling in opposite directions (180° out of phase) will cancel each other. The cardioid microphone is usually of the dynamic or condenser type, although there are also combinations of dynamic and ribbon or condenser and ribbon.

The frequency response and range of a microphone vary according to its design and function. It is desirable to have a very smooth frequency response over

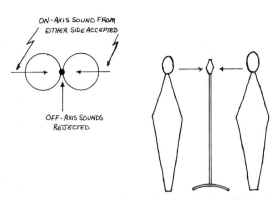

Fig. III–10   *Polar response pattern of a bidirectional (ribbon) microphone.*

whatever frequency range is necessary for your purposes; that is, the frequency response should not vary by more than 2 or 3 db up or down. If there is a rise in the low frequency response the microphone will sound boomy; a rise at the high end will make the sound "brighter" (Fig. III–13). These colorations may be desirable for certain effects, but it is better to have an uncolored microphone that records sounds accurately, and be able to add the coloration later with an equalizer. A tall narrow peak in the frequency response will also color the sound and may cause severe feedback problems if used in a public-address or reinforcement system. The desirable frequency range depends on the function of the mi-

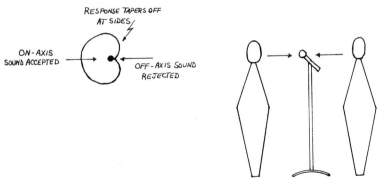

Fig. III–11   *Polar response pattern of a cardioid (directional) microphone (the term "cardioid" comes from the heart-shaped polar response pattern).*

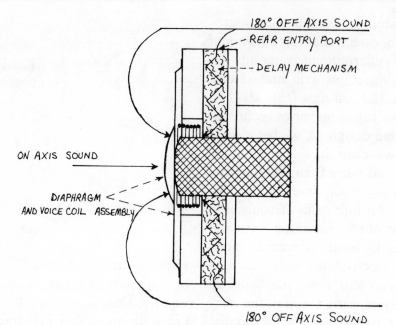

Fig. III–12 *Cross section of cardioid microphone showing rear entry ports and delay mechanism* (after Burroughs).

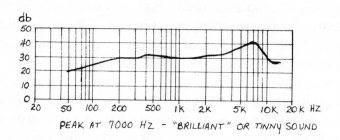

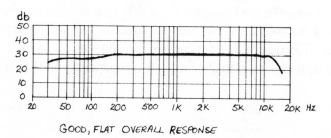

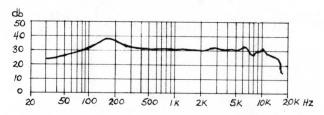

Fig. III–13 *Some typical microphone frequency response curves.*

crophone; for music recording you will want a fairly wide range (say 40–18K Hz or wider), whereas for voice-overs you would need a narrower range (100–12K Hz). Some microphones come with switches labeled VOICE/MUSIC, which control the bass response to vary the frequency range. When you want to record only speech you can attenuate the low frequency response and eliminate excess low frequency noise, keeping the speech clearer and brighter. Other microphones have a bass boost or attenuation switch, which adjusts the frequency response below 100 Hz either up or down 10 db (Fig. III–14).

Microphones are classified as high impedance (Hi-Z) or low impedance (Lo-Ƶ). A high-impedance microphone has an output impedance of anywhere from 1,000 to 50,000 ohms (usually 30,-000 to 50,000). It should be used with a short cable; any excess cable length (more than 20 or 30 feet) will cause attenuation of the signal. Needless to say, a high-impedance microphone can be used only into a high-impedance mic input, either on a tape deck or a mixer. High-impedance microphones are generally not used in theatre work because of the limited cable length; they are still used with some of the less expensive home tape recorders and cassette recorders. Low-impedance microphones usu-

ally have one of four output impedances: 50 ohms(Ω), 150 ohms, 250 ohms, or 600 ohms. Some microphones may have an interchangeable output impedance; it is a simple matter of rewiring one lead from the 250Ω terminal to the 50Ω or 600Ω terminal. Low-impedance microphones may be used with long cable lengths (200–300 feet) with little or no attenuation. At low impedance levels, slight mismatching of microphone impedance and amplifier input impedance will have little noticeable effect, although pairing a 600Ω microphone with a 50Ω input and vice versa would produce noticeable gain or loss in level and possibly a change in frequency response. Most low-impedance professional microphone wiring is balanced; that is, a separate carrier is used for grounding. A balanced microphone has a three-pin connector and uses two conductor shielded cable. Pin 1 is the ground and is connected to the cable shield; pins 2 and 3 carry the audio signal, and their phasing (which pin goes to which wire) may differ among manufacturers. An unbalanced microphone has only a two-pin connector and uses single conductor shielded cable. The shield carries both the ground and one side of the audio signal. Actual wiring diagrams and adapters are shown in Appendix II.

The output level of microphones varies among types and designs. Generally

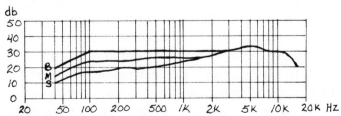

Fig. III–14 *Frequency response curve of microphone with bass attenuation switch. Bass, Medium, and Sharp positions adjust bass response to suit individual needs.*

speaking, low-level microphones (−58 to −62 db) are used for close work while high-level microphones (−48 to −52 db) are used for distance work. Low-level microphones are frequently used for rock music and other extremely loud sound to prevent overloading the preamplifier. Many microphone preamplifiers now come with attenuation switches at the connector to step down the level by 10 or 20 db.

Microphones are not indestructible; they need the proper care and maintenance that all delicate instruments require. Dynamic microphones are less susceptible to ill effects from temperature and humidity extremes than are condenser types. When working outdoors or in extremely humid conditions, try to use a dynamic-type microphone. All microphones should be protected as far as possible from dust and particles. Although many microphones have dust filters, these can become clogged if exposed to dust under pressure, and this will seriously affect frequency response. When testing a microphone *do not blow into it.* This will force dust into the microphone and the moisture of breath and saliva will cause loose dust to stick to the filter or to the diaphragm itself. Dynamic microphones, with their permanent magnets, are particularly susceptible to ferric dust (metal), so be wary of carrying them out onto the stage just after the crew has finished cutting pipe or welding. Condenser microphones are adversely affected by moisture, so store them in a dry place (preferably not too hot). Also, be sure to remove the battery between uses so there will be no corrosion of contacts. Ribbon microphones are in some ways the most delicate. The amount of tension in the ribbon is critical to its operation, and that tension can be changed by someone's blowing into it at close range. (The ribbon may stretch.) Also, such a loud, sharp sound as a gunshot may stretch or even tear the ribbon. Some general rules for care of microphones are: never blow into them from close range; avoid areas of heavy dust concentration, particularly ferric dust; and when not in use keep microphones in boxes or cases in a cool dry place, or, if they must remain on their stands, cover them with cloth dust covers.

MIXERS AND AMPLIFIERS

An audio mixer enables the sound technician to mix several input signals into a single output signal. A stereo mixer permits mixing various input signals in any combination into two separate output signals. Each input position has a continuously variable attenuator control, so that the level of any individual input signal may be changed without affecting the others. A multiple output mixer (stereo, 3-channel, 4-channel, etc.) has some form of switching at each input position to allow any input signal to be fed to any output channel. Usually there is a sub-master control for each output channel. Since current technology has made miniaturization not only possible but economically feasible, modular components are becoming standard in mixer design. Plug-in cards at the inputs permit a choice of line level or microphone preamplifiers; these cards are interchangeable, so that the mixer can be used for all line level inputs or all microphone inputs or any combination. Modular technology permits custom design of mixing consoles; the sound engineer can get exactly the number of inputs and outputs needed at that time and still have the possibility of future expansion. Miniaturization means that several components whose size had previously relegated them to a separate equipment rack are now included in the mixing console—most commonly equalizer circuits. The only caution concerning current solid-state mixers is that they cannot always be used with older tube-type equipment because of impedance mismatching (see Chapter II).

The kind of power amplifier needed depends on how the system is to be used. For a recording studio a stereo power amplifier, or a separate power amplifier for each channel, is needed solely for monitoring purposes. It should be powerful enough to reproduce sound effects at a realistic level without distortion (that is, at the approximate decibel levels at which they will be heard in the theatre). If you have efficient speakers and a small studio, 30 or 40 watts per channel should be sufficient. In a reproduce system in a small theatre a single power amplifier per output channel should be sufficient (or a stereo power amplifier for a two-channel system). If there are no more than four speakers in parallel (of nominal 8Ω impedance), their combined impedance (with all four speakers driven by the same channel) will be 2Ω. If the speaker switches are wired from the 4Ω tap of the amplifier, the impedance mismatch will not be too serious. In most cases you can avoid having all four speakers driven by one channel by sending the inputs to both channels of the mixer and having two speakers switched to each channel. Another solution is to use nominal 16Ω speakers so that even with all four speakers run off one channel the total impedance is down to only 4Ω. In a large re-

produce system with six or eight or more speakers, it is advisable to have a separate amplifier for each speaker. With solid-state technology this is not difficult or bulky; however, it is still more expensive. The amount of power necessary from an amplifier is still a disputed question, but whatever amplifier you choose, it should be able to produce 100 db continuously through your system, with peaks of 110 or 115 db, without distortion.

Amplifiers should be mounted in a cool place, if possible, and in such a way as to allow maximum ventilation. An amplifier produces a great deal of heat, and if this heat is not allowed to escape, the build-up will activate the thermal breaker, designed to protect the unit from overheating. If there is no thermal breaker, serious damage can be done to the transistors by the excess heat. Care should be taken to protect the amplifier from dust and dirt, as these may clog ventilation ports and cause overheating. It does not hurt to clean an amplifier with a gentle vacuum cleaner if it does get dirty. With proper care a solid-state amplifier should last at least ten years.

LOUDSPEAKERS

The function of a loudspeaker is to convert electrical energy into acoustical energy. The method and the accuracy with which this is done varies among manufacturers. For use in the theatre, a speaker should give the most accurate reproduction possible to assure the sound designer that the sound he created is the sound the audience will hear. More than any other piece of audio equipment, the speaker tends to "color" the sound it reproduces. Some of this coloration can be seen as dips and peaks in the speaker's frequency response curve (Fig. III–15), but there are other forms of sound coloration and distortion in speakers that cannot be recognized just by reading the specifications and looking at response curves. In fact, speaker specifications, unfortunately, tell us very little about what a speaker will actually sound like. First of all, it is very difficult to tell from a percentage number just what kind of coloration will be produced by inter-modular and harmonic distortions. (Intermodular distortion occurs during the

frequency increases. Many speaker manufacturers have compensated for this by providing several high frequency drivers (of very small dimension) or by using deflecting elements in their speaker systems. The facts remain, however, that no two speaker types sound alike and that while one speaker may sound the most "true" in one room, a completely different speaker will sound most "true" in another room because of the effects of the room acoustics.

Some explanation of terminology may

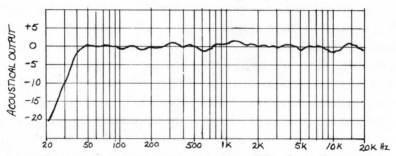

Fig. III–15 *Typical speaker frequency response curve (taken free-field on axis).*

interaction of two sound waves of different frequencies being reproduced by the same speaker. Harmonic distortion is the production of sound at frequencies harmonic to the fundamental frequency; in other words, if the sound to be reproduced is 2000 Hz, the speaker may also produce some sound at 4000, 6000, or 8000 Hz.) Second, the total sound image of a speaker is dependent on reflected sound from the room environment as well as on direct sound from the speaker. How much reflected sound there is at different frequencies depends on the po-lar pattern or directionality of the speaker system. Almost all speakers have omni-directional bass response, but re-sponse becomes more directional as the

be necessary at this point. The term "speaker" may refer either to a single, individual unit (also known as a *driver* or *radiator*) or to a *speaker system.* A speaker system consists of two or more drivers within a single enclosure. These drivers are of different sizes (and some-times of different types) and reproduce different frequency ranges. The sound signal first goes through a *splitting net-work* or *crossover network,* which passes only high frequencies to the high fre-quency driver ("tweeter"), only low fre-quencies to the low frequency driver ("woofer"), only mid frequencies to the mid frequency driver, and so forth for as many drivers as are in a particular speaker system.

There are several types of speaker design. The most common (because it is simple, inexpensive, rugged, and has a fair degree of fidelity) is the *electro dynamic* speaker. In principle this speaker is just the reverse of the dynamic or moving-coil microphone. It consists of a coil suspended in a magnetic field and attached at one end to a cone or diaphragm. Pulsating electric current fed to the coil by the amplifier causes the coil to be pushed back and forth by the magnet. This motion is transferred to the cone, which in turn pushes the air in pulsating waves (sound waves). This is the basic principle; many refinements have been developed over the years to increase bass response, to smooth out the overall frequency response, or to lower the percentage of harmonic and intermodular distortions. These refinements have to do with size of the driver, cone stiffness and mass, and enclosure design. Of the non-dynamic type speakers, the *electrostatic* is becoming popular as a mid and high frequency driver to be coupled with a dynamic type bass driver. The electrostatic speaker is in principle essentially the reverse of the condenser microphone. It consists of a fixed metal grid (counterpart of the plate in the microphone) that has a constant electrostatic charge, and a flexible metalized plastic diaphragm.

The voltage from the amplifier is applied to the diaphragm, causing it to be attracted and repelled by the constant polarization of the grid. The motion of the diaphragm transfers the electrical energy into acoustical energy. The frequency response of the electrostatic speaker is much smoother than that of the dynamic, but because of limitations of the size and excursion of the diaphragm it is practical for reproducing only the mid and high frequencies.

Most commonly, speakers have a "nominal impedance" of 8 ohms, though there are also nominal 4-ohm and 16-ohm speakers on the market. The "nominal impedance" is simply what the manufacturer states is the impedance of the speaker. In some cases it has little to do with the actual impedance, and there is as yet no industry standard for rating speaker impedances. The impedance of a speaker varies with the frequency of the signal, with the highest impedance appearing at the bass-resonance frequency of the speaker (Fig. III–16). Usually there is a dip in impedance right after the resonant frequency peak, and this has become a common point at which to rate the speaker impedance (the lowest impedance measured immediately after the bass-resonance peak). Other speaker manufacturers arbitrarily assign an "av-

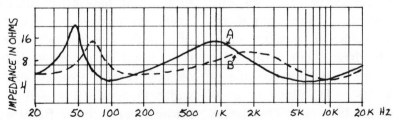

Fig. III–16 *Impedance curve of two typical speakers. Although both speakers have similar maximum, minimum, and average impedances, speaker A has a manufacturer's rating of 4 ohms whereas Speaker B (from a different manufacturer) is rated at 8 ohms.*

erage" impedance rating (usually 8 ohms, even though the actual range is from 4 to 18 ohms). All this would seem to be of little importance, since the impedance does not affect frequency response, distortion, or any other measurement of quality. The only thing it does affect is the amplifier. The lower the impedance, the more current is drawn from the output stage of the amplifier, and at a certain point the output transistors will suffer damage (usually below 2- or 3-ohm loads, although some amplifiers will remain stable as low as ½ ohm). Most amplifiers have built-in protective circuits that will turn the amplifiers off before such damage occurs. Apply all this to the theatre in which the sound engineer tries to drive eight speakers with one amplifier, and you can see the problem. If they are 8-ohm speakers, the amplifier is seeing a load of 1 ohm, and chances are, even if they are rated as 8-ohm, the speakers reach low impedance levels of around 4½ or 5 ohms at some frequencies, which puts the load well below the area of safe operation. (The impedance, Z, of a number of speakers connected in parallel is computed as follows: $\dfrac{1}{A} + \dfrac{1}{B} + \dfrac{1}{C} + \ldots \dfrac{1}{N} = \dfrac{1}{Z}$ where A, B, C, and N are the impedances of the individual speakers.)

Some mention has been made in previous sections of speaker efficiency and power requirements. It should be remembered that less-efficient speakers need more power to drive them, and that a reproduce system should be capable of putting out a 110- to 115-db sound pressure level without distortion. This means that the speakers must have a large power-handling capacity, as they may be driven, at peaks, by 150 watts or more. It is debatable whether theatre speakers should be fused or not. A large burst of power could seriously damage a speaker if it does not have fuse protection, but on the other hand, it would be very inconvenient to have speaker fuses blowing during a performance. If your theatre speakers are fused, make sure the fuses are large enough that, while protecting the speaker from severe damage, they will not blow from loud sound cues. It should be noted that certain types of sound will damage speakers more easily than others—primarily very low frequency sine waves. This should be remembered particularly in the recording studio when playing with a sine wave signal generator; the ear is less sensitive to low frequencies, so if you are sending a low frequency signal through the system, the tendency is to turn up the volume—*don't*. A 12-inch speaker cone must make an enormous excursion to try to reproduce a 30-foot sound wave. The higher the volume, the larger the excursion of the cone, and eventually it will be pushed beyond its limits.

Auxiliary Equipment

A good theatre recording studio will have such extra equipment as equalizers, reverberation units, and sound generators. These may all be part of an electronic synthesizer, or they may be separate units. The function of an *equalizer* is to boost or attenuate individual frequency bands, usually one octave in width. Generally it is used to compensate for peaks and dips in frequency response resulting from room acoustics or equipment characteristics, but for theatrical purposes it is also used to change and distort sounds when creating certain effects. (This is discussed in Chapters IV and VII.) Equalizers are available with a variety of band widths and curve shapes. If money permits, a recording studio should have one with the narrowest band and sharpest curve possible, to permit filtering out of specific unwanted frequencies without affecting the overall sound. Most mixers for reinforcement and reproduction systems have some type of equalizer in them; in less expensive systems they are simple high and low pass filters similar to the bass and treble controls on home stereo units. These filters are there primarily to compensate for room acoustics and frequency response characteristics of the system.

Several types of reverberation and echo devices are available, and any one is appropriate for a recording studio, depending on what type of sound is desired. Perhaps the most common is the *spring reverberation* unit, which consists of several coiled metal springs. A sound wave travels more slowly down a spring than it does through air, so a specific amount of delay can be obtained in this manner. Usually spring reverberation units have several springs, of which two are used to carry the signal and the others to balance the mechanism of the active two. A sound wave is transmitted to the first spring, travels down it, and is reflected back up it; at the top of that spring is a bridge to transmit the signal to the second spring. The wave travels down the second spring to a pickup, where it is converted from mechanical energy back into electrical energy. Not all of the wave is absorbed by the pickup, however, and the rest is reflected back up the second

spring and transmitted to the first spring, where it starts its journey all over again. This process continues until all the energy is dissipated or absorbed. The major disadvantage to the spring reverberation unit is that the sound is colored by the natural reverberation characteristics of the springs, although this problem has been reduced in high-quality units by means of damping.

A more expensive but much more realistic sounding device is the *steel plate* reverberation unit. This consists of a large steel plate in close proximity to, but not touching, a fiberglass damping plate. A signal is applied to the steel plate by means of a driver, similar to a dynamic speaker but without the diaphragm. A pickup unit—a crystal contact microphone—placed a specific distance away on the plate picks up the signal and the successive reflected signals. In a stereo unit there are two pickup units spaced to pick up different reflective patterns. This type of unit produces a reverberation sound similar to that obtainable in an echo chamber. For this reason it is an ideal unit for adding ambience to music and sounds recorded in a dead studio, as well as for creating special sound effects.

When a studio lacks any separate reverberation unit, it is always possible to create an echo effect on any multi-track, multi-channel tape deck. Some decks are equipped with echo function switches that make the job easier; in this case, refer to the tape deck manual for instructions on how to use the echo mode on that particular deck. On decks not equipped with this special feature, it is still possible to produce some echo. This is accomplished in the following manner: Record the source sound on track one.

Connect the outputs of both channels to separate inputs of a mixer, but putting both mixer inputs through the same mixer output channel. (This combines both output signals from the tape deck, but allows separate volume control.) Connect the mixer output to the Channel Two input of the tape deck. Put Channel Two *only* in the record mode. Put both channel monitor switches on "tape" or "reproduce" so that you are monitoring from the playback head. The distance from the record head to the playback head will determine the time delay of the echo. The Channel Two input volume control will determine the general strength of the echo, the Channel One output volume control will determine the strength of the initial echo, and the Channel Two output volume control will determine the amount and strength of successive echoes. The Channel Two output volume control must be used with great care, and you should start off with a *very low* reading on this control. If too much signal goes from the Channel Two output back to the Channel Two input, the deck will go into self-oscillation (an interesting effect, but not what you were trying to achieve in the area of reverberation).

Several kinds of *signal generators* are available. Wave form generators (also known as oscillators) produce particular wave forms over a broad frequency range, preferably in the sweep format rather than a stepped frequency determination. The most common wave forms are the sine and square waves, and frequently one generator will produce both of these wave forms. Other generators produce sawtooth, triangle, and trapezoidal wave forms. There are also white noise generators and generators that produce noise of varying degrees of "color." (White noise is noise containing every frequency of the audible spectrum, in the same way that white light is said to contain all the colors of the light spectrum. Colored noise contains many random frequencies, but not every frequency. A cymbal crash, for instance, is noise only at the high end of the spectrum.) All types of signal and noise generators are useful in the recording studio; they are the basis of electronic sound and music, and are the central component in an electronic synthesizer. The advantage of having signal generators as part of a synthesizer rather than as separate units is that a synthesizer uses voltage-controlled oscillators or generators so that one oscillator may be controlled by the output of another as a function of either frequency or amplitude (Chapter I).

Noise Reduction and Compression/Expansion Units

The best-known type of noise reduction unit is the Dolby B; this is the Dolby unit that appears on many high-quality home stereo components. The principle of the Dolby B unit is very simple: low-level signals of high frequency (1000 Hz and above) are boosted by 10 db immediately before recording; then in playback the same frequency range is attenuated by 10 db, bringing that portion of the original source sound back into balance with the rest of the signal. In the process any high frequency noise that was not in the original signal, but was added during the recording (i.e., tape hiss), is reduced by 10 db—this means a very clean, quiet tape. There are two drawbacks to this system. First, it is a noncompatible system; that is, any tapes recorded with Dolby-encoded noise reduction must be played back through a Dolby unit, and tapes that were not encoded should not be played back through a Dolby unit. Second, the Dolby unit is limited to reducing noise introduced in the recording process; it can do nothing to reduce background room noise or scratchy record noise, and it cannot help a noisy old tape that was recorded without Dolby.

Another type of compression/expansion unit for noise reduction is manufactured by the firm *dbx*. It is more complex than the Dolby B unit and requires proper adjustment for good results, but since it works across the entire audible frequency range it is effective against hum and other low frequency noises as well as tape hiss. This unit works on the principle of dynamic range compression and expansion. Weak signals coming into the unit are amplified or compressed. (Strong signals are untouched, because any amplification of them might cause tape saturation and distortion, and these signals are loud enough to mask noise anyway.) In playback, the dynamic range is expanded to what it was originally—that is, those signals which were boosted in the compression process are attenuated to their original levels—and, of course, any noise introduced between compression and expansion is also reduced by that amount. This unit has the same disadvantages as the Dolby: noncompatibility and limited field of effectiveness.

Two other forms of noise reduction are currently available, and both are open-ended; that is, they do not require encoding and decoding, but work to reduce noise already existing on a tape or record. The dynamic filter is a low-pass filter (one that passes low frequencies but not highs), which has an on and off action controlled by the level and frequency content of the signal passing through it. If the signal is loud enough to mask noise, the filter is switched out, so that all frequencies pass. If the signal is too weak, or if there are no high frequencies in the source signal, the filter is switched in, reducing high frequency noise. There are two problems with this: it does reduce high frequencies in the source signal as well as noise—that is, the filter has an audible effect on the program content; and quite often there is an audible swish of noise when the filter cuts out. But in the more sophisticated dynamic filters these problems have been reduced to a minimum, and the units can be quite effective.

The newest type of open-end noise reduction system to hit the market is called the autocorrelator. This system distinguishes between the specific frequencies of a music program and random noise energy. If a signal is present at any fundamental frequency below 2000 Hz at a level higher than the background random noise level, then a series of gates open up to pass that fundamental frequency and its multiples or harmonics up to 20,000 Hz. All the other gates remain closed (unless there is a signal to open them), blocking random noise. This system is good for music, but not necessarily for sound effects, since many sound effects would be read as random noise.

TYPES OF RECORDING TAPE

In the open-reel format there are three types of recording tape: standard, low noise, and low noise/high output. These are all ferric oxide tapes—that is, the magnetic material on the recording side of the tape is gamma-ferric oxide. (Tapes made with chromium dioxide and cobalt-doped ferric oxide are used primarily in cassettes and so will not be discussed here.) Each type of tape requires its own particular bias and equalization settings for optimum performance. Three conditions must exist for optimum performance: minimum distortion, maximum but smooth high frequency response, and maximum signal-to-noise ratio. Unfortunately, there will always be a compromise among these three factors because the bias setting that will produce minimum distortion will also produce a significant drop in high frequency response. This is compensated for, to some extent, by the record equalization setting; the high frequencies are boosted somewhat in the recording process to offset the drop produced by the bias settings. There is a limit, however, to how much the highs can be boosted before creating an overload in either the tape or the electronics of the deck.

Because of these compromise conditions, tape manufacturers are constantly looking for ways to improve tape. These improvements are usually in the form of better high frequency response, and thus better signal-to-noise ratio, higher overall output levels, and higher saturation point. These are accomplished by the use of smaller and more tightly packed ferric oxide particles, better magnetic orientation of the particles, and improved binders for adhering the particles to the tape base material. Each of these changes and improvements will, of course, change the optimum bias and equalization settings

for the tape, so it is particularly important in a recording studio to choose one type of recording tape, set the bias and equalization curves of your tape decks for optimum performance with that tape, and then use that tape consistently for recording. (Since the bias and record equalization affect only recording, not playback, you needn't worry about playing other types of prerecorded tape.)

The type of tape you choose will depend on the kind of work you do and the size of your budget. Needless to say, the low noise or low noise/high output tapes will give better performance, but they also are more expensive. If you do any sizable amount of recording you should buy tape in bulk, a carton (12 reels) or a case (48 reels) at a time; you can get a better price this way. Also there are many tape discounters around the country who do mail-order business. If there is a reliable one in your area, by all means use him. For convenience you may want to buy tape on 7-inch reels, but you can save money by buying 10½-inch "pancakes" and running the tape onto smaller reels as you need it. There are other choices to be made about tape besides performance characteristics and price: tape thickness, for instance. A thickness of 1 mil will give you more recording time per reel, but it is more difficult to edit. If you are recording long pieces of music that will not have to be edited, then 1-mil tape may be what you want; if, on the other hand, you primarily do sound-effects tapes for shows, or if you have inexperienced students working with the tape, then 1.5-mil tape is recommended. Another choice is whether you want an acetate- or a mylar-base tape. Mylar tends to age better, not cracking or becoming brittle under extreme temperature changes. Acetate, however, has the advantage of breaking cleanly under tension, making it possible to repair a broken tape. Mylar will stretch as much as 100 percent before breaking; once a tape has stretched it can never be repaired.

No matter what tape you use, certain procedures will give you extended life and better performance. Tape should always be stored in a cool, dry place. Acetate-base tape in particular may curl at the edges or become brittle, and even mylar-base tape is subject to some deterioration in adverse conditions. Tape should always be wound smoothly on the reel; an uneven winding, such as you get in fast forward or rewind on many machines, will produce curled edges after a while. If a tape is not flat it will not make complete contact with the heads as it passes across them, creating an uneven dropout effect. Avoid touching the magnetic surface of the tape with your fingers; oil from the skin will also produce dropouts. Any kind of dirt on the magnetic surface of the tape will not only cause dropouts, but also create an abrasive surface against the tape heads, shortening their life considerably. Any kind of magnetic field in close proximity to a recorded tape can cause high frequency loss or partial erasure, so avoid contact with speaker magnets, head degaussers, and the like.

If you expect to get top performance from your sound systems over a period of time, proper care and maintenance are as important as choosing the right equipment initially. A system that *looks* good will usually be handled with more respect than a sloppy system that has temporary mountings and jerry-rigged wiring, especially in a studio that is used by many different people.

Chapter IV

DOING SOUND FOR A THEATRICAL PRODUCTION

THE CONCEPT, THE DIRECTOR, THE SOUND COLLAGE

The first steps in doing sound for a show are reading the script and meeting with the director. Before meeting with the director, it is important to be familiar with the script and to have a general idea of the sound requirements. The director may, of course, want something completely different than what is described in the script, but you, as the sound designer, should have some ideas of your own. You should attend all "concept" meetings with the other designers, particularly if the show is being conceived in an unusual way. At some point you and the director must get together and discuss, in terms of the show's concept, what the *sound collage* will be.

The sound collage is for the sound designer what fabric swatches are for the costume designer. You must determine the texture of sound that will best suit the show. Sometimes a show will be done with a variety of sound textures, but usually you will want a style that will give a unity to the sound score (and will be unique to that show). I speak of this style and texture in broad terms, of course. Do not misread me to mean that all the cues should sound alike for a particular show; but there should be a unifying factor that

associates a cue with that particular sound score. Just as scenery and costume designers have various ways of unifying their designs—color, texture, style, period—so you have similar means—tone color, sound texture, style of treatment.

There are five broad styles of theatrical sound, within which there are as many variations as there are sound designers. The five are:

1) Realistic sound effects made by recording the real thing.
2) Pseudorealistic effects that sound real but were made from other sources.
3) Musique concrète—nonrealistic sounds created from a variety of sources, used in their natural state or electronically distorted. This montage of sound creates a musical type of sound background.
4) Electronic, synthesized sound effects, either realistic or nonrealistic.
5) Live sound.

The first step in arriving at a sound collage is to choose the style, or combination of styles, that suits the show and its production concept. For example, in a modern production of a Shakespeare tragedy (say *Macbeth* or *Hamlet*) your styles might be pseudorealistic and musique concrète. A word of caution: it is wise for the novice sound designer to stick with one or two styles for a particular show; a combination of more than two styles can produce a muddy and uneven sound score.

The next step is to choose your source sounds; that is, the types of sounds you will begin with to create your effects—musical instruments, human sounds, and sounds of glass or wood are just a few examples. Again, for the sake of unity, it is often wise to limit yourself to a few types of sound sources (although you must also take care that the score does not become monotonous). Sound sources and treatment of sound are discussed more fully in the next chapter.

Once you have understood the production concept of the show and decided on a sound collage with the director, you must then return to the script to find specific cues. There are five categories of cues you should be looking for and several ways to obtain each effect, depending on the style you have chosen for the show.

USES OF SOUND IN THEATRE

1) *Realistic Effects Called for in the Script.*

These are usually nature sounds (birds, thunder), people sounds (footsteps, knocking at the door), and specific music cues (radio, phonograph, Albert playing the piano in the next room). They can be done live, or on tape unchanged, or on tape distorted. The first two methods are self-evident and need no further discussion, except that they should be as clean and realistic as possible. Distorted realistic sounds are useful for indicating an emotional or mental state of a character or for denoting an external supernatural influence on the scene. A simple distortion of size or volume of a sound can be an effective tension builder. (Such sounds as a heartbeat, a clock ticking, or footsteps built louder and louder can create suspense or horror.)

2) *Voiceovers.*

A common use of sound in theatre is the voiceover—off-stage voices that need amplification; machines that talk; apparitions, witches, and weird beings. The simplest form of voiceover is done with a live microphone backstage. If the voice is to be that of an actor in the show who is not on stage at the time of the cue it is better to do it live, because the actor will have a feel for the audience and the pace of the show that particular night. If, for any reason, the actor cannot do the cue live, then it must be put on tape. Frequently a voiceover cue requires distortion. A certain amount of this can be added to live mic cues through a reverb unit and the equalizers in the playback system. But, if a lot of changes have to be made in the voice quality, it is best to do it on tape.

3) *Punctuation Effects for Entrances, Exits, Ends of Scenes.*

There are times when sound is not specifically called for in the script but when a certain sound will make an effective punctuation at that point in the script. A director will often want to accent an entrance or put a button on the end of a scene. Sounds that accomplish these fall under three categories.

a) Realistic Effects—A door slam

may mark an entrance, and, of course, we have thunder to bring on the witches. Realistic punctuation sounds are usually of a short, sharp, and percussive nature.

b) Musical Punctuations—Either live or taped music is frequently used in a show. Percussion instruments can be used as accents; fanfares punctuate entrances and exits; and a musical "tag" brings a scene to a decisive end. If there is no musical composer working on the show, you will have to turn to classical music for fanfares and tags. (Be careful of using contemporary pieces; you might have to obtain permission from the holder of the rights.) For percussive effects, either live or taped, simply hire a relatively accomplished percussionist and have him improvise. One caution when using live percussion—make sure the cues are finally set before opening, so that your actors are not surprised by new and different sounds every night (unless, of course, that is precisely what the director has in mind).

c) Electronic and Abstract Sounds— This category is limited only by the sound designer's creativity. If you are fortunate enough to be at a university that has an electronic synthesizer (or working on a show with a large enough budget to rent one), then lock yourself up with it for five days and you should come out with enough usable material. Actually the synthesizer is extremely useful for creating punctuation sounds—stings, boings, zaps, honks, and clunks. If you don't have access to a synthesizer, don't despair. You can create some very fine punctuation sounds from wood, stone, metal, musi-

cal instruments played unmusically, and the electronic things you can do in any ordinary sound studio. The important thing is to make the sound work as an accent to a scene. Once again, the most effective sounds are sharp or percussive, although this is not a strict rule.

4) *Underscoring for Mood or Character Themes.*

This is perhaps the most difficult type of sound cue to design successfully. It is often the first thing to be cut in a tech rehearsal. This may seem surprising, since it is a technique that works so effectively in movies and television. But in live theatre underscoring is usually more of a distraction than an aid, primarily because of balance problems and focus. In films and television the sound mixer rides gain on the background sound track so it is always correctly balanced to the voice track. In live theatre it is rarely possible for a sound operator to be in a position to ride gain according to how loud the actors are, and it is difficult to set specific up and down cues since actors have different timing and projection every night. Even at low levels, background sound can be distracting because the audience has such a broad image to focus on. The movie or television camera does the focusing for us visually, making it possible for background sound to be present but not distracting because we know from the visual scene what we must focus on. This having the camera do half our work for us has, I fear, produced a lazy generation of theatregoers. This is proved by the fact that virtually all current Broadway musicals are amplified— not because today's voices are weaker but because today's audience concentration has slipped drastically.

Now that I have begun this section with the necessary cautions, let me say that underscoring is possible and can be very effective if done carefully. Usually you will want to fade the cue out very gradually once it has been established, not play it through the entire scene.

a) Realistic Effects Underscoring —Usually realistic effects are used to establish a mood, a place, or a weather condition: the creaking of an old house, sounds of the city streets, or rain on a tin roof. Occasionally realistic sounds may be used as a character theme, such as strong wind accompanying the statue in *Don Juan.*

b) Musical Underscoring—If you intend to use a lot of music to set moods in a particular show, it would be wise to hire a composer or at least an arranger. Classical music pieces may work for some things, but there is a limit to how far they can be bent to fit the mood you want. Also, most serious musical compositions were created to stand on their own; rather than serving to enhance a play, they distract from it by being a new element for the audience to listen to. A good theatrical music composer will supply an open-ended piece of music that will create the right mood and support the play without being a self-contained piece needing separate attention. If you cannot hire a composer you may find just the music you need in recordings of film scores, but you must, of course, acquire permission to use it.

Musical character themes are generally of a simple nature—either a melodic theme played on different instruments or in different keys depending on the disposition of the character, or a single instrument playing different simple themes. However it is done, it should be easily recognizable and readily associated with that character; then later in the play you can use the theme to indicate the influence of that character on what is happening even though he is not present.

c) Electronic and Abstract Sounds— The only limitation on this type of underscoring is to make sure it is not distracting from the scene. It may take you a long time to find exactly the right sound, however, since the sources are nearly unlimited. The process of creating and choosing these sounds is discussed more fully in the next chapter.

5) *Preshow Atmosphere.*

Preshow sound can be used to prepare an audience for a show. Realistic effects will establish a place or weather conditions—sea gulls, waves lapping the shore, rain, wind, or thunder. Recorded music might establish a particular country, period, class, or mood. When electronic sound or musique concrète is used in a show, a preshow tape will not only set a mood but also introduce this type of sound to the audience. It is important to acquaint the audience with strange sounds before the play begins, so that they will not be distracted by the first few cues. There are times, of course, when you want the audience to be taken by surprise with a sound cue, and these particular cues should not be previewed.

It should be mentioned that, whenever necessary, historical research should be done. This may be necessary for a show such as *Oh What a Lovely War,* where the sounds of explosions, guns, airplanes, and war machines should be World War I vintage. It is often necessary to research period music, as well. This kind of research should be done in the planning stages before your work starts in the studio.

THE SOUND PLOT AND WORK SHEETS

Before you actually begin work on creating the sound cues for your show, it is advisable to organize your work on paper. First, you should get together with the stage manager and do a sound plot (Fig. IV–1). The stage manager can be very helpful in giving you precise placement of cues and timings for them. He will also inform you of any changes in script or concept as rehearsals progress.

The last step before going to the sound studio is to do a work sheet (Fig. IV–2). You will save yourself many hours of aggravation if you plan things in advance.

Know what types of source sounds you will need; it is best to do several sessions of source recordings before you start your mixes. For complex mixes, know which combinations you want on what track. Certain sounds can be properly balanced in the studio, but others can be balanced only in the theatre with the actors—these sounds must be left on separate tracks. Also, you may want certain sounds to be separate, so they can come from different speakers. You should plan in advance the setup of the cues for easiest running operation. If you have a series of identical cues put them on one deck so the mixer need be preset only once for the whole sequence, even if there are intermediate cues on the other deck. Know ahead of time whether a cue should have a built-in fade or whether the operator can do it. The more you have planned in advance, the fewer times you will have to redo cues. You'll have to redo enough as it is—don't make more work for yourself.

PAGE #	CUE #	DESCRIPTION	TIME	DECK	TRACKING	SPEAKERS
1	0	Joyous Carillon	:40	B	I & II	All
12	1	Ugly War	1:00	A	I—Rifle, Machine Gun II—Screams, Explosions, Fist Fight, Animal Fight	Stage House
	1A	Additional Explosions	:50	B	I & II	House
16	2	Bugle Call	:05	B	I	Stage
17	3	Whistle Explosion	:08	A	I—Whistle II—Explosion	Stage
17	4	Whistle Explosion	:08	A	I—Whistle II—Explosion	Stage
21	5	Gentlemen's War	:30–:40	A	I—Marching Troops II—Bugle Calls, Cheers	Stage House
21	6	Fanfare	:25	B	I	Stage

Fig. IV–1 *Sound plot for Yale University production of Ionesco's* Macbett.

CUE	MIX — TRACK I	MIX — TRACK II	SOURCE SOUND	TREATMENT	NOTES
0	*1812 Overture Carillon—stereo*		*Commercial record*	*None*	*Build beginning on tape*
1	cannon shot		pistol shot (record)	½ speed	
	machine gun :05		machine gun (record)		
	:04 X-FADE				
	surrealistic machine gun		typewriter (live)	slow down, filter out highs	
		fist fight ⌐ :05	Joe and Mike (live)		
		cat & dog fight ⌐ :12	Carol (live)		
	explosions :45	:15	explosions (record)	slow down, reverb	
		man falling down stairs	Joe—Vernon Hall stairs (live)		
		moans & groans	Joe & Mike (live)	slow down slightly	
		glass crash	bottle hit with hammer over cardboard (live)		
		glass being swept up :32	glass swept around on cardboard (live)		
	scream :05		Mike (live)	reverb (?)	
	fire		paper crumpled (live)	slow down, reverb	
	grunts & breathing :10		Joe & Mike (live)		
	scream :07		Joe (live)		
	cannon shot		pistol shot (record)	½ speed	

Fig. IV–2   *Work sheet for* Macbeth.

Chapter V

RECORDING TECHNIQUES

THE STUDIO

Although it is not always possible, because of spatial limitations, to have an ideal recording studio in a theatre situation, there are ways to make the best of what you have. If possible, the studio should be a double room separated by a "soundproof" wall with a window in it (Fig. V–1). (I put the word "soundproof" in quotes because the amount of sound that the wall must block is not great, so that even an ordinary double fiberboard wall with a 3-inch airspace should be adequately soundproof.) One room of the studio will house all the equipment and should be large enough to allow comfortable working space for several people. The other room should be an acoustically variable recording room; the variations

can be obtained by movable panels or drapes. There should be at least one movable acoustical panel in the room to provide separation when discrete stereo recording is needed. Built into the dividing wall between the two rooms should be a junction box for microphone connectors on the recording-room side with leads going to the equipment patchpanel. As has been previously mentioned, fluorescent lights should not be used in the recording room, because they will cause a 60-cycle hum; be aware also that air conditioner and ventilating fans can cause unwanted noise in recordings. If a double-room studio is not possible and the equipment must be in the same room as the live sound source, then the equipment must run quietly or you will have to use carefully placed directional micro-

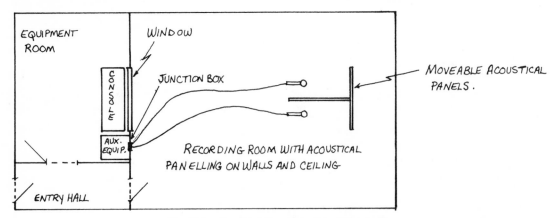

Fig. V–1 *Simplified floor plan of recording studio.*

phones to avoid having equipment noise in the background of your tape.

When setting up the equipment in a studio the major concern is operational ease. (Ventilation of certain equipment is also important, but that is more a question of how it is mounted than where it is mounted.) The control console or mixer is, of course, the central piece of equipment, and in addition to mixing facilities it should contain tape deck remote-control switches and monitor speaker control switches. At least one tape deck should be mounted in a horizontal position near the control console. (This is more for editing purposes than recording.) The turntable should be mounted separately from any other equipment (to prevent accidental jarring during recording), but it should be near enough to the console to allow the operator to reach the tape remote switches while operating the turntable. Auxiliary equipment can be rack-mounted but should be convenient to the console. Any tape decks that are vertically mounted should be at such a height that the heads are easily accessible. The console should be at a height convenient for standing or sitting on a medium-height stool (to accommodate both preferences of work style). The top of the console should be not so high as to block the view over it.

Dubbing Records and Tapes

The simplest type of recording is duplicating or "dubbing" prerecorded records and tapes. A straight dub can usually be done by going directly into the tape deck, bypassing the mixer. Assuming there is a patchpanel, this would be done by patching from "Phono out" to

"Tape in" of the deck to be recorded on, or, if it is a tape to be dubbed, from "Tape I Out" to "Tape II In." The outputs of the recording deck would then be patched into the mixer inputs in order to monitor the sound. The owner's manual should be consulted for proper operation of your particular tape deck since each brand is slightly different, but I shall describe the basic recording procedure that should apply to any deck (Fig. III–1).

1) Put recording tape on the left-hand spindle of the machine, threading it properly past the heads and between the capstan and pinch roller, and winding it firmly onto the take-up reel.
2) Switch the machine out of "safety" into "ready record."
3) Switch the monitor switch to "input" or "source."
4) Turn input selector switch (if there is one) to "line" position.
5) Turn playback volume controls up to a moderate level (around 6 or 7 on a 10 scale).
6) Turn record volumes up to a low moderate level (4 or 5 on a 10 scale).

You are now ready to set proper recording levels. This is simply a matter of playing the source sound (record or tape) and adjusting the record volume controls on the recording deck until you have the correct meter readings for the particular type of sound you are recording. At this point a word about meters is necessary. Any deck to be used in a recording studio should be equipped with a standard professional VU meter calibrated to industry standards. It will read numerically from −20 to 0 in black and from 0 to +3 in red. A meter reading in the red does not necessarily mean distortion; in fact, on any properly aligned professional deck using high-quality tape, distortion will not occur until beyond +3 VU. The one problem with meters is that they are slow-acting compared to the instantaneous peaks reached in music and sound, so they often will not register a peak that is at distortion level. For this reason many machines now have an LED (light-emitting diode) peak indicator in addition to the meter. This enables the recording engineer to record at the highest possible levels without distorting. If your machine does not have LED peak indicators, you must keep the record level within the +3 VU limit of the meter or risk distortion on peaks.

All this does not mean that every type of sound should be recorded at the highest possible level. Proper record levels vary among sounds and music. Experience provides the best rules for what level is right for what sound, but I shall list some general hints that seem to work best in theatre recording.

1) *Music.*

Classical music generally has a wide dynamic range. The average loud passage should register around 0 VU so that peaks do not exceed +3. Soft passages will register as low as −7 or −10 and should not be boosted if proper dynamic range is to be maintained. If only a short segment of music is to be used and the entire segment is quiet, it may be desirable to boost the level to around −3 VU, but remember that in boosting the level of the music you also boost the level of background noise already on the source

record or tape. Other types of music (rock, folk, and popular) generally do not have such a wide dynamic range. Rock music should be recorded at the highest possible level without distortion if it is to sound right when played back. Folk and popular music will probably fall within the −5 to +1 range on the meter.

2) *Spoken Voice.*

Average speech (neither yelling nor whispering) should usually register between −7 and 0 on the meter. Yelling, of course, will peak up to +3 VU (unless it is meant to be distant as a special effect). Whispering, if it is to be reproduced as normal whispering, will read as low as −10 or −15. If it is recorded much higher than −5, it will not sound natural in reproduction.

3) *Sound Effects.*

Obviously loud sounds such as thunder, gunfire, car crashes, and anything else that the director will want reproduced at a loud level in the theatre should be recorded at the highest possible level before distortion. Any effects that are to be reproduced realistically should be recorded at natural levels: footsteps, for instance, may read only −10 to −7; twittering birds or crickets will also register low on the meter.

Normally, you will want to record sounds and music with their natural dynamic range. One exception to this rule is if the sound or music is to be played as a background to a scene. In this case, the dynamic range should be compressed or flattened a bit so that the entire passage is at roughly the same level; otherwise, if the playback level is loud enough to hear the quiet sections it will be too loud, drowning out the actors, on loud sections.

During the recording process, a certain amount of rough editing can be done that will save time later and may even save a generation in the recording process. The key to saving time and limiting the number of dubs necessary to obtain a finished cue is planning ahead (see Chapter IV). If you know in advance that a cue should have a built-in fade-up at the beginning and/or fade-out at the end, these can usually be done on the first dub from the record or tape. If the cue is a piece of music but the sections are to be used out of sequence, then record them out of sequence rather than having to reorder the tape in the editing process. If only certain arbitrary sections of a long sound cue or piece of music are to be used, don't record the entire work, but stop the deck between those passages to be used. These may seem like very simple and basic procedures that should not even have to be included in a textbook such as this, but even experienced sound designers have wasted time, tape, and energy by not planning ahead and not using these very basic techniques.

LIVE RECORDING

The solutions to the problems of setting up for a live recording session (number of microphones, their type and placement, room ambience, etc.) are as numerous as sound engineers and recording studios. Each engineer will solve the problems in his own way, according to the particular recording situation and the kind of sound desired. There are few, if any, hard and fast rules about what microphone to use when, how close it

should be to the source, and how many microphones should be used in a particular situation. Whatever works best for you in your studio is the "right" solution, and the only way to find it is through experience and experimentation. As a guide to that experimentation, I shall discuss some of the methods and solutions that have worked for me in recording theatrical sound effects.

The simplest effect to record is the single voiceover—an actor recording a speech for playback during a performance. The solution to this recording problem depends on the final sound quality desired: does the director want it straight and dry, or with some natural reverberation, or should the voice sound as if it's in a huge stone cathedral? For a straight, dry recording (little room ambience) a directional microphone, preferably high-output, should be used. With a high-output microphone, the actor can stand at the proper distance and speak in a normal voice while the input gain can be set low enough that not much background noise or room ambience will be picked up. This applies to what are known as Single-D (single-distance) microphones. Many cardioid microphones are Single-D and have an optimum working distance of about 2 feet. Unwanted variations in the frequency response will occur at other distances, giving an unnatural timbre or sound quality to the voice. If a Variable-D directional microphone that will accept a working distance of 3 to 6 inches is available, that will give you the cleanest, driest voiceover with little or no background noise and room ambience. If a certain amount of ambience is desired, it is best to use an omnidirectional microphone. If your studio is equipped with reflective panels, these can be arranged to produce the desired amount of ambience. If a hollow, cathedral-like effect is desired, you can, of course, find a large reverberant room (a church, or the stone-walled corridors of a school), use portable equipment, and record the natural reverberation with omnidirectional microphones. Or, if this is not feasible, you can make a studio recording, filter it, and add reverberation to suit your needs. If a director isn't sure what he wants to do with a voiceover effect, it is best to record it by the first method; reverberation and frequency changes can always be added to a dry recording, but they cannot be removed if they are recorded into the source tape.

To set up for multiple voiceovers or choral sound effects, the same rules apply for obtaining a dry or an ambient recording, but now you have the added complications of multiple microphones and whether they will all go into one channel for a monaural recording, or into two or four channels for a stereo or quadraphonic effect. If the effect is a simple dialogue (or any verbal interaction) between two actors, it is best to use one microphone per actor and a separate tape track for each microphone. That way you have a stereo effect if you need it, but it can always be mixed down to one channel in playback if that is desired. If both microphones are to be put through the same input channel, they should be placed several feet apart and arranged so that each microphone is picking up only one actor's voice; otherwise you may experience phasing cancellation effects. If one actor is standing between two microphones (both going to one channel) but he is not precisely equidistant between

the microphones, then the sound waves of his voice will reach the closer microphone before they reach the farther one, creating two identical wave formations but slightly out of phase with each other. When mixed together the phase difference will cause partial cancellation. (See Chapter I.) Choral effects using several actors can be recorded with one omnidirectional microphone, with the actors being placed in a semicircle or "V" in front of it, or in stereo with two smaller groups of actors around two separate microphones (Fig. V–2). For the stereo record-

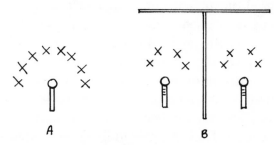

Fig. V–2 *Microphone arrangements for recording choral effects.* A: *Monaural, using one omnidirectional microphone.* B: *Discrete stereo using two cardioid microphones separated by acoustical panel.*

ing, if you wish discrete channels, you should use cardioid microphones separated by a panel; if the stereo effect is being used merely to add dimension to the sound and need not be discrete, then omnidirectional microphones may be used. For some choral effects you will want a stereo recording in which the sounds move between the two channels; this is simply a matter of having the actors move between two microphones that go to two different channels of the tape deck. If it is a large group of actors and you use more than one microphone per channel, be sure to separate them to avoid phase cancellation (Fig. V–3). You

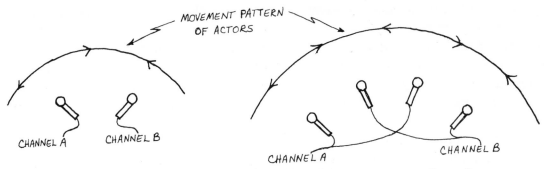

Fig. V–3 *Microphone arrangements for stereo moving choral effects. Some phase cancellation effects may be noticeable depending on the type of microphones and their spacing; however, that effect may be desirable— listen and experiment.*

may have to do several experimental takes to determine the correct spacing and direction of the microphones to provide the kind of sound flow you want. (For a smooth transition from channel to channel, the microphones must be spaced so that there is no drop-off in pickup of one before the actor moves into range of the other.) You may find, occasionally, that "bad" recording techniques (such as placing the microphones in a phase-canceling situation) will produce interesting and usable effects. If so, go ahead and use the distortion as an effect. Fortunately, in the business of theatrical sound effects, anything goes, as long as the final sound is what the sound designer and director want.

For recording "mechanical" effects, the main considerations are whether the sound should be monaural or stereo and how much background noise or room ambience is desired. Obviously a mono recording will require only one microphone, whereas a stereo recording will use two. Experimentation is the best way to determine the correct distance of the microphone from the source sound for each particular effect. If the sound is to be created by striking one object with

another (such as a chime struck with a mallet), you may wish to keep the microphone fairly distant so that the sound of the actual strike will not be predominant. To record a door slam, the microphone should be far enough away to catch the natural room reverberations of the slam and not pick up too much of the clicks of the doorknob and latch, which would not sound realistic if they were too loud. If the desired effect is not meant to be a realistic sound, then a closer microphone position may prove better. The only caution about recording mechanical effects is in regard to damaging the microphone. A very loud, explosive sound could be too much for a microphone to handle at close range; watery effects should be recorded with care that the microphone itself does not get wet; and effects that raise dust should be recorded with a wind screen or some other filter for protection.

The most complicated area of recording is live music. Even for recording a single piano, microphone placement is critical; the microphones must be close enough that the sound is not muddy, but distant enough not to pick up the mechanical noise of the keys and pedals. To some extent microphone placement is a matter of taste. Some engineers prefer the clear, sharp, sometimes bright sound of a close microphone position; others prefer the richer, more blended sound of a more distant microphone. Of course, if you are working with single-D microphones, it is best to position them at their optimum working distance (usually about 2 feet) in order to maintain a flat frequency response. The question of whether to use an omnidirectional or cardioid microphone is also a matter of taste and of experimenting with each new recording situation. If you are using microphones for reinforcement and may run into feedback problems, then cardioids may be the answer; or if you know you want a dry recording with a high degree of separation between channels, choose cardioid microphones. You should keep in mind, however, that there are certain disadvantages to using cardioid microphones—they are less apt to have a uniform, flat frequency response, they are more susceptible to high-level distortion, and they more easily transmit handling and shock noises because their cases tend to be microphonic. Omnidirectional microphones tend to reduce these problems, and, for the same quality reproduction, are usually less expensive than cardioid microphones. All this discussion is simply meant to prompt the sound engineer to experiment in each new recording situation to decide for himself what type of microphones will produce the particular sound quality desired from that recording session.

The problems of recording increase with the number of instruments to be recorded and the number of microphones used. Too many microphones will often create new problems and produce a worse recording than too few. For the purposes of recording an orchestral piece for use in the theatre, the method that is easiest, fastest, and least likely to fail is to do a simple stereophonic recording using two microphones suspended head-to-head above and in front of the orchestra (Fig. V–4). Arrange the orchestra so that the louder instruments are in the rear and the softer ones in front. If more separation is desired and it is necessary to use more microphones, then apply the three-to-one ratio rule to your microphone setup: the distance from one microphone to the next microphone must be three times the distance from the microphone to the sound source (in this case the musical instrument). This ratio is the minimum one at which phase distortion seems to be inaudible. If you wish to mic each section of an orchestra separately but a particular section is too big to be handled by one microphone, then use the head-to-head principle with two microphones to cover the area (Fig. V–5).

Mixing and Overlaying

In addition to being able to set up microphones correctly and capture a sound

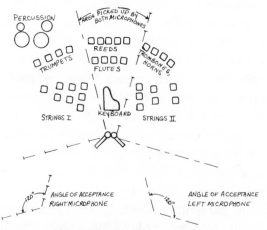

Fig. V–4 *Microphone and orchestra arrangement for simple, nondiscrete stereophonic recording.*

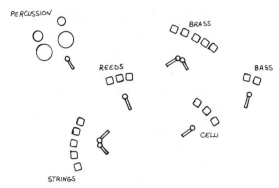

Fig. V–5 *Microphone and orchestra arrangement using separate microphones for each section.*

with the desired amount of ambience, the sound engineer must record the sounds in the best tracking configuration and with a good balance. The first step in this process is to work out in advance which sounds in a complex mix must remain on separate tracks (either for a stereo effect or to allow final balancing in the theatre) and which sounds can be mixed together in the studio. Refer to Chapter IV for a more complete explanation of the work sheet. Usually when there is a complex sound cue to be made, the individual source sounds are recorded separately and then are either mixed together two at a time or, in the case of a studio with a four- or eight-track machine, overlaid track by track. The more tracks you have available, the fewer generations of tape you will have to go through to arrive at your final mix, and the fewer generations, the better the sound quality. Referring to Cue 1 on the work sheet for *Macbett* in Chapter IV, I shall explain the process for making a mix of fifteen different sounds. If you are working only with two half-track tape decks the following procedure would be used:

1) *Record All Source Sounds on Track I of Deck A.* (Actors Mike and Joe were recorded with two micro-phones mixed through the mixer into one track doing the fistfight, moans and groans, and grunts and breathing. The cat-and-dog fight in this case had to be done on two tracks because one person did both the cat and the dog; the dog was recorded on Track I, the cat overlaid on Track II, then the two tracks were mixed down to one.)

2) *Treat All Source Sounds to Arrive at What Each Should Sound Like.* Knowing that the pistol shot would be played at half speed to become cannon shots, I recorded it originally at 15 IPS so that I could then use the original source tape played at 7½ IPS and not lose a generation. Other source sounds, such as the typewriter, the moans and groans, and the paper crumpling I knew would take experimentation to find the correct playback speed, so they were recorded at 7½ IPS and then dubbed from a variable-speed tape deck at the best sounding speed. In the case of the typewriter, the filtering was done in the same dub as the slowing down. (Track I Out from the variable-speed deck was patched to Equalizer In; Equalizer Out went to Track I In of the other tape deck. When the proper speed and filtering were arrived at, the dub was made.) In the case of the explosions and the paper crumpling, the reverberation was added in the same dub as the speed change.

3) *Make Sure All Sounds Are Long Enough.* In the case of source sounds recorded live, you would simply record a long enough segment to begin with. In the case of

a sound taken from a record or a tape where the original is not long enough, you would either make several dubs initially and edit them together before treating the sound, or you could record the sound only one time through initially, make several dubs during the treatment stage, and then edit them together. The choice is whichever sound will be easier to edit—treated or untreated. In the case of a speed change, the faster version is usually easier to edit.

4) *Lay in the Sounds That Will Eventually Mix Down to Track I.* Put a fresh tape on Deck B. Dub the cannon shot from Deck A onto Track I of Deck B. (Make sure you take out the record volume before stopping the machine at the end of the dub to avoid getting any clicks on the tape, since you will not be able to edit them out with other sounds on the opposite track.) Now cue up the machine-gun source on Deck A and cue up Deck B to just before the end of the decay of the cannon shot, which is now on Track I. Take Track I *out* of the record mode into safety and put Track II into record. You are now ready to lay in the machine-gun sound on Track II, overlapping it just barely with the tail end of the cannon shot decay. You know in advance that you want five seconds of machine gun alone, then about four seconds more as the typewriter sound fades in under it, then a three- to four-second fade-out. So you will dub nine seconds of machine gun onto Track II at a loud level, then fade

it out in a three- to four-second fade. When this is done, cue up Deck A to the treated typewriter sound and cue up Deck B to five seconds into the machine-gun sound on Track II. (If it is essential to have precise timing, Deck B should have a self-synchronization feature. That kind of precision is usually needed only for music, however, and not for sound effects.) Be sure, of course, to switch Track II out of record and Track I into record. You will now lay in the typewriter sound on Track I, making a four-second fade-up at the beginning and letting it run for forty-five seconds. This done, cue up a little way into the typewriter sound and lay in the explosions on Track II. The explosions, in this case, end before the typewriter sound, so the scream will also go on Track II, timed to come right at the end of the typewriter sound. (Since the scream lasts five seconds, it should probably overlap the last second or two of the typewriter and then go three or four seconds in the clear.) Looking ahead, you will see that the second scream should overlap both the fire sound and the grunts and breathing sound. This means that you will have to do a premix of the fire with the grunts and breathing. Remove the main mix tape from Deck B and put on a blank tape. Lay in the fire sound on Track I. It will last about ten seconds and fade out fast. The grunts and breathing will begin three or four seconds into the fire sound and go onto Track II. They will fade out with the fire sound. Now take this new tape of both sounds, put it on Deck A, and replace the main mix tape on Deck B. Cue up Deck B to the end of the scream—there should actually be a second of silence after the scream before the fire sound begins. Now, going through the mixer, dub the fire, grunts, and breathing, mixed through one output channel, onto Track I of Deck B. You will then dub the second scream onto Track II, beginning in the last two seconds of the fade-out of the fire and breathing mix. The final cannon shot will go onto Track I after a second of silence after the scream. (Note the importance of planning ahead; if you realize that you will have to make the premix of the fire with the grunts and breathing *before* you begin making the Track I master, it will save you the time and bother of inserting that step in the middle. If I had realized it before I began writing "Step 4" it would have saved me writing half a paragraph!)

5) *Put Aside the Finished Tape for Track I of the Final Mix and Lay in the Sounds That Will Eventually Become Track II.* The same procedure is used. The fistfight will go onto Track I, overlapping with the cat-and-dog fight on Track II. (The cat-and-dog fight source tape, being on two tracks, will have to be mixed down onto Track II in this dub.) The cat-and-dog fight continues past the end of the fistfight by about eight seconds, during which the man falling downstairs is laid in on Track I. At the end of the cat-and-dog fight leave three seconds of silence, then lay in the moans and groans on Track I. The glass crash and glass being swept up will go onto Track II during the first fifteen seconds of the moans and groans. (The moans and groans will last a total of thirty-two seconds.) That completes the tape for the final Track II.

6. *To Make the Final Mix Down,* put a blank tape on Deck B and the Track I master on Deck A. Patch Deck A Outputs through the mixer, putting both through output Channel I. Patch Channel I Output into Track I Input of Deck B. Make a dub, being sure to balance any overlapping sounds. Then recue Deck B to the beginning of the Track I dub and set up to record on Track II. Put the Track II master tape on Deck A and repatch the Channel I Output into Track II Input of Deck B. You're now set to lay in the final Track II mix. The first sound on Track II will begin twenty seconds after the beginning of the Track I sound. This should time out so that the moans and groans on Track II end at the same time as the fire, grunts, and breathing on Track I. Again, be sure to get a proper balance on any overlapping sounds on Track II as you make the final dub. Balancing the final Track I to Track II will be done in the theatre.

If you are fortunate enough to have a four-track or eight-track deck, you will be able to lay in all the sounds for this cue on one master, since there are never more than four sounds occurring simultaneously. The premix of the fire with the grunts and breathing would be unnecessary.

Methods of Changing Recorded Sound

In theatrical sound work the sound designer is inevitably called upon to change or distort original sounds to create the desired effect. Chapter VII treats more fully the questions of when and why sounds should be distorted and what the final effect of any particular change will be. In this chapter I shall discuss the methods of distortion and how to accomplish them. The three simplest methods which require no extra equipment are changing the speed of a sound, making a dub of the sound backwards, and mixing the sound with another. Most professional decks are two-speed machines. This means that a sound can easily be played back at half speed or at double speed. Assuming that the final playback speed (in the theatre) is 7½ IPS, if you want a sound reduced to half speed you would simply record the source sound at 15 IPS then play it back in the theatre at 7½ IPS—no further dub would be necessary. If you wish the final sound to be twice its normal speed, you would either record it initially at 3¾ IPS (if you have that option) and play it back at 7½ IPS with no further dub necessary, or you would record the source sound at 7½ IPS, then make a dub playing the sound at 15 and recording at 7½. The pitch of the sound will change proportionately to the speed. A dub at half speed will be one octave lower than the original, and a dub at twice the speed will

be one octave higher. With a variable-speed machine you can make a dub at an intermediate speed and you can vary the speed during the dub (sweeping from slow to fast to slow and so on to create a warbling effect or doing a slow build from slow to normal and back to slow to create the Dopler effect.) To have a sound reproduced backwards, you simply edit it into the show tape in the reverse direction. Mixing sounds must also be considered a method of treatment and distortion. Incompatible sounds, when mixed, will interact with each other, causing acoustical cancellation and reinforcement and intermodular and harmonic distortions. Also, it is sometimes desirable to mix a source sound with a dub of itself at half speed. The techniques of mixing and overlaying are discussed earlier in this chapter.

With auxiliary equipment, sounds can be extensively changed or distorted. The two most useful auxiliary pieces in a sound studio are a filter or equalizer and a reverberation unit (or, lacking that, echo capabilities within the system). As was discussed in Chapter III, a recording studio should have a filter with a narrow band width (no wider than one octave) and a sharp curve (preferably 16 db per octave). The filter should be equipped with a bypass switch so that you can do direct A-B comparisons of the filtered and unfiltered versions of the sound. For convenience and flexibility, there should be one filter for every output channel of the system; a stereo unit with separate controls is fine for a two-channel system, two stereo units for a four-channel system. The filter inputs and outputs should appear at the patchpanel so that it can be inserted anywhere in the system. (In other words, you should be able to patch individual tape decks or phono outputs into the filter and the filter into the mixer; or, if your patchpanel is set up with a "special effects insertion" section, you can insert the filter into any of the mixer inputs without tying up the mixer outputs.) Basically the use of the filter is quite simple: you boost or attenuate various frequency bands according to what sound you want as the final result. Some filters have variable cutoff slopes, and you should consult the instruction manual for your particular model.

A small or medium-sized recording studio should be equipped at least with a spring reverberation unit. If you can afford a steel-plate type, so much the better. A stereo unit is ideal, but if you cannot afford it, a mono unit is better than none at all, and possibly you can add another mono unit in a few years. If you are lacking any auxiliary reverberation equipment, refer to Chapter III for a description of how to produce an echo effect within the system. If you have a custom mixer, chances are it has echo send and return controls on it. These controls should include a switch to determine where the signal is picked off to be sent to the reverb unit—the choices being before the mixer volume control, after the mixer volume control but before special-effects insertion, or after special-effects insertion. In the first position, the reverberation signal will appear at the echo return control even if the volume control of the original signal is all the way out. This means you *can* record only the reverberation signal if you wish, or mix in as much or as little of the original "dry" signal as you want by means of the mixer volume control. In the second po-

sition, the signal being sent to the reverb unit is controlled by the mixer volume control as well as by the echo send control. This means that the signal appearing at the mixer outputs will include both dry and reverberation signals. If you have the filter inserted into the circuit through the special-effects insertion jacks at the patchpanel, the third position of this switch allows you to send the signal to the reverb unit after it has been filtered. This is particularly handy for combining filtering and reverberation in one step. If your system is very simple and does not have these extra capabilities, it is always possible to patch the tape or phono outputs into the filter inputs and the filter outputs into the reverb unit inputs and the reverb unit outputs either into the mixer or into the other tape deck inputs. Once the reverberation unit is inserted into the system, its use is straightforward: by means of the controls provided, add as much or as little reverberation as is necessary for the sound you want.

Two other more sophisticated types of treatment are possible with other pieces of equipment. A ring modulator is a device which, when fed two signals of different frequencies, will produce the sum and the difference of those two frequencies but neither of the original frequencies. In other words, if the inputs received two sine waves of 430 and 610 Hz respectively, the output would produce a signal of 180 Hz and 1040 Hz. Any sound can be fed into the ring modulator and modulated by any other sound. It is usually wise, however, to begin with a simple tone as the modulating signal if the sound effect to be modulated is complex. With two complex signals fed into the modulator the output could get confused and muddy.

A phase shifter is a device that can intentionally create phase distortion and cancellation effects electronically. With this device you can vary the phase difference of two signals from 0° to 180°. Two identical signals may be sent into the phase shifter to reproduce a third distorted signal in whatever degree desired. A phase distortion effect can be reproduced without a variable phase shifter by simply making up a patch cord that is 180° out of phase. (See Appendix II for wiring diagram.) A stereo signal (in which the two tracks are similar but not identical) can be sent through the mixer, one track through a regular patch cord and one through the reverse phase patch cord to produce partial phase distortion. In this case, if the two signals were *identical* there would be complete cancellation, making the process useless. However, one can create a "stereo" signal out of a mono one by putting the mono signal through two outputs of the mixer, sending one output through the filter, changing it in some way so that it is no longer identical to the original signal, and reversing the phase of one of the two signals. The result will be partial phase distortion.

Chapter VI

EDITING TECHNIQUES

PREPARING THE EQUIPMENT FOR EASY EDITING

One deck in every studio should be mounted in a horizontal plane with enough work space in front and to the sides to allow for easy editing. The splicing block should be permanently mounted on the flat surface in front of the deck (Fig.VI–1). (Some people prefer to mount the block on top of the deck's head-block assembly, but this usually does not provide enough flat surface for comfortably resting the hand when cutting and applying splicing tape, and it also increases the danger of getting small scraps of tape into the head-block assembly and deck transport.) The splicing block should be a solid metal block with a quarter-inch-wide groove running the length of it (to hold the recording tape) and two razor-blade-width slits for cutting, one at 45° and one at 90° (Fig. VI–1). [The so-called hourglass splicer

Fig. VI–1 *Editing deck, showing splicing block and editing materials.*

85

that includes a press bar with built-in razor blades and makes an hourglass-shaped splice (Fig. VI–2) has several disadvantages and is not preferred.] Although the 90° cut can be used to edit

Fig. VI–2 *Hourglass splice.*

sounds with very sharp attacks, in most cases the 45° cut is preferred because it makes a stronger splice. For this reason, the splicing block is usually mounted with the 45° cut to the left and the 90° cut to the right (Fig. VI–1). With the splicing block permanently mounted, you can now measure off a cue mark for easy editing. It is unwise to mark a tape directly on the playback head, because it will promote dirt and excess wear on the head; but there is usually a convenient place to mark the tape somewhere to the right of the playback head on the head-block assembly. Usually the farthest-right tape guide is in such a position as

to allow easy marking without even removing the head-block protective cover. This is the preferable place to mark. Now simply measure the distance between that tape guide (or other marking spot) and the center of the playback head. (Thread a piece of tape onto the machine, make one mark at the tape guide and one mark at the center of the playback head.) Then transfer the measurement to the splicing block, placing the playback head mark directly on the 45° cut of the block and making a permanent mark on the block (or on the flat work surface) where the tape guide mark is on the tape. From here on, you will always mark your tape at the tape guide and place that mark on the permanent cue mark you have made on the splicing block (Fig. VI–3).

The basic materials needed for editing are the splicing block, splicing tape, wax marking pencil, razor blades, and leader tape. The splicing block has already been discussed. Correct splicing tape is the next most important item in the editing process. For ¼-inch-wide tape it is pref-

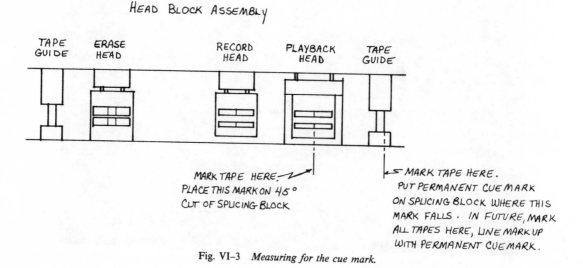

Fig. VI–3 *Measuring for the cue mark.*

erable to use either $\frac{3}{16}$-inch- or $\frac{7}{32}$-inch-wide splicing tape. The $\frac{1}{4}$-inch-wide splicing tape will inevitably produce some overhang of splicing tape over the edge of the recording tape; this, when wound on the reel, will stick to the next layer of tape, causing uneven feeding and more rapid deterioration of the tape over a long period of time. If a great deal of editing is done in your studio, it is advisable to have a tape dispenser for the splicing tape (Fig. VI–1). This makes the job faster and easier. However, if the splicing tape is not used over a period of several days or weeks the dispenser may prove wasteful, as that tape which is exposed to air for an extended period will lose its stickiness and will have to be discarded.

Leader tape comes in a variety of types and colors; what is preferable depends on each studio's uses and needs. Paper leader tape is less susceptible to holding a static charge and is therefore quieter, but it is generally not considered to be strong enough for use in show tapes (although it may be preferable for master tapes). Plastic leader tape is generally used for show tapes; it comes either opaque or translucent, with timing marks or without, and in white or a variety of colors. The only caution about choosing leader tape is that a translucent leader tape will activate any automatic cueing device that runs on a photoelectric cell. In that case opaque leader tape must be used except for those places where it is desirable to stop the machine by the automatic cueing device. For convenience it is usually preferable to purchase leader tape on 7-inch reels. You may find it possible to have a peg or a hook close to the editing deck on which to put the reel of leader tape for easy dispensing.

Single-edge razor blades are a standard item that can be purchased anywhere. (For obvious reasons double-edge blades are not recommended!) The rough use it will get on the editing block will cause any blade to wear out quickly, so it is not worth the extra money to buy "good" blades. It is usually less expensive to buy them in bulk, and you will go through them rapidly enough to make that worth while. It is not advisable to use a dull or a nicked blade; the cut will be ragged and uneven and the butted joint will not match properly, making a noisy and weak splice. Wax marking pencils or "grease" pencils are the standard markers for editing work. The mark applies easily and can be wiped off once the splice is made. Felt-tip markers and ball-point pens are not recommended, because certain types of ink will eat through the tape; rather than take a chance on getting the wrong ink, avoid them entirely.

SPLICING

Good splicing, like any other manual skill, takes practice. With time and practice you will develop your own particular style of splicing that is easiest for you. Any method is "correct" as long as the finished product is right. I shall set forth the method that has worked best for me.

1) *Finding the Sound.*

If you are looking for the beginning of a sound cue, run the tape at normal speed until you hear the beginning of the sound. Stop the deck. You are now a short way into the sound (if your reactions are good, perhaps only a second or so). You must now jockey the tape back and forth across the playback head by hand, to find the precise beginning of the sound. Most decks have some form of editing mode that will defeat the tape lift mechanism and allow the tape to pass across the playback head without engaging the transport in the play mode. Some machines may also have a reel motors on-off switch that allows one or both reels to be free-wheeling without tension. I prefer to maintain tension on the reels while editing, but some people do not—purely a matter of personal taste. Once you have put the machine into the edit mode so that the tape will make contact with the playback head when you move the reels by hand, you must then jockey the two reels back and forth slowly, listening for where the sound begins. It

takes a little training of the ear to determine what sound is what at such a slow speed, but with a little practice it should become easy. Even in the beginning you will be able to distinguish "silent" tape from sound. By jockeying the tape back and forth, find the precise point at which the silence ends and the sound begins (Fig. VI–4). Leave the tape in this position with the beginning of the sound right on the playback head. Mark the tape at your designated marking point on the back or nonmagnetic side of the tape.

2) *Transferring the Tape to the Splicing Block.*

Make sure that your hands are clean and oil-free and that the splicing block is clean. By hand rotate both reels to the inside (Fig. VI–5) to unwind enough tape to reach the splicing block comfortably.

Fig. VI–4 *Find the sound by jockeying the reels back and forth.*

Take the tape by the *edges* (avoid putting your fingers on the magnetic or recorded side of the tape) and place it in the groove of the splicing block, backside up. (That is, the nonmagnetic side should be up, leaving the recorded side face down against the block. This used to mean that the shiny side should be up, but this is no longer always the case since some of the newest types of tape have a dull backing coating, making the magnetic side shinier than the back of the tape.) Adjust the tape so that the mark on the tape is lined up with the cue mark on the splicing block, and secure the tape by pressing it into the groove.

3) *Overlaying Leader Tape.*

Assuming you are working on the beginning of a cue and wish to splice leader tape to the beginning of the sound, the next step is to lay the end of the leader tape over the recording tape in the groove of the splicing block so that about ½-inch of leader tape extends to the left of the 45° slit (more is unnecessary and wasteful) and the rest of the leader tape extends to the right of the 45° slit (Fig. VI–6). When joining a piece of leader tape to a piece of recording tape (or joining two pieces of recording tape), it is best to cut both pieces at once so that the abutting ends will be matched.

4) *Cutting the Tape.*

Taking a sharp razor blade, make a single, clean cut through both leader and recording tape into the 45° slit of the splicing block (Fig. VI–7). I usually place the end of the razor in the slit above the tape and draw it through from top to bottom. Some people prefer to rest the

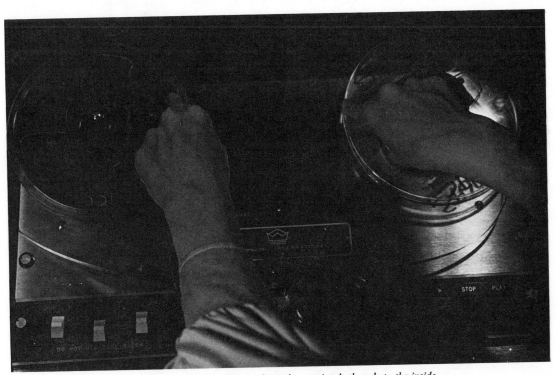

Fig. VI–5 *Unwind a length of tape by rotating both reels to the inside.*

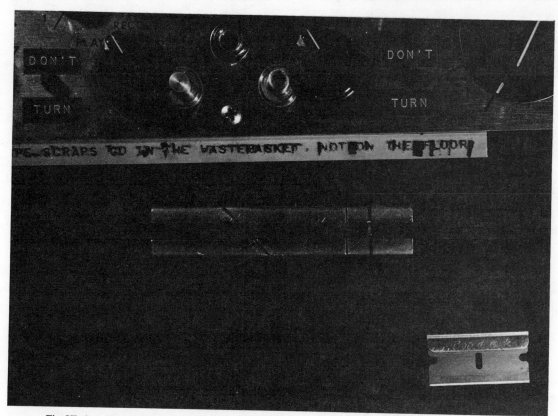

Fig. VI–6a *Place tape in splicing block, lining up the two cue marks (one on the tape and one on the block).*

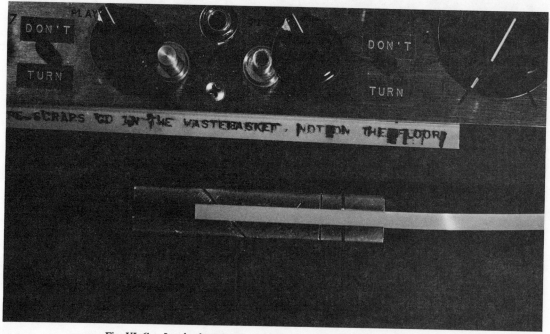

Fig. VI–6b *Lay leader tape over recording tape in the splicing block groove.*

Fig. VI–7 *Cut both leader and recording tape together through the 45° cut of the splicing block.*

entire blade edge over the slit and press down through the tape. Either method works as long as it is done in a single clean motion. It is important, of course, that both the recording tape and the leader tape are secure in the groove to provide tension against the cut, and that your razor blade is sharp and free of nicks.

5) Butting the Ends.

Once the cut is made, remove the left-hand scrap of leader tape and the right-hand excess recording tape (under the leader tape) and discard them properly. (Tape scraps on the floor make a messy studio, and a messy studio promotes sloppy workmanship.) Then with your fingertips slide both leader tape and re-cording tape (still in the groove) to the right until the freshly cut ends lie in the middle of the block between the 45° and 90° slits (Fig. VI–8). This is so that the area to be joined will be over a solid section of the block and not over a slit. Carefully butt the two ends together so that there is no overlap and no space between. If you made your cut sharp and clean this should be possible.

6) Applying the Splicing Tape.

Take a piece of splicing tape about ¾ inch or 1 inch long and carefully lay it over the joined ends, parallel to the groove so that the splicing tape does not ever run over the edge of the recording or leader tape. If the splicing tape does overlap the edge of the recording tape,

Fig. VI–8 *Butt the newly cut ends together in the middle of the splicing block.*

Fig. VI–9 *Apply splicing tape across the joint and rub it on, to secure it.*

you will have to trim the excess with a razor blade after you remove the tape from the splicing block. If you use $\frac{3}{16}$-inch or $\frac{7}{32}$-inch splicing tape, there should be some space on either side between the edge of the splicing tape and the edge of the recording tape (Fig. VI–9). You will have to experiment to find which method of holding the splicing tape works most easily and accurately for you. I have fairly narrow fingers and have found a way of holding the edges of the splicing tape between the thumb and third finger and using the outer edges of the splicing block as a guide for straight alignment. Larger fingers may find this method awkward. Once the splicing tape has been laid over the joint you must then secure it; a fingernail will usually do the job, or the covered, safety edge of the single-edge razor blade (used with care, of course). Ideally, there should be no air bubbles under the splicing tape.

7) *Removing the Tape from the Block.*

There are two cautions for this step in the splicing process. First, don't touch the recording tape on the magnetic side; handle it by the edges. Second, remove the tape from the groove carefully so that the edges of the tape do not curl. I have found that the best method of removal is to take the tape (by the edges) at both ends of the splicing block and pull gently both upward and outward (Fig. VI–10). The tape should pop out of the groove with no damage to the edges. Once this

is done, wind the tape by hand onto the feed reel (left-hand reel), thread it properly and run it through once at the correct speed (both to secure the splice and to enable you to check your work).

The finished splice should have a perfectly matched joint (with no overlap or gap), should have no air bubbles under the splicing tape, should have no splicing tape overlapping the edges of the recording or leader tape, and should be at the precise beginning of the sound to be edited. (Fig. VI–11). The same procedure would be used to attach leader tape to the end of a cue. You would find the precise end of the sound (including its natural decay), mark it, and place it in the splicing block. When applying the leader tape, in this case, the ½-inch excess

Fig. VI–10a   *Hold tape by edges on either side of splicing block, being careful not to touch magnetic side of tape.*

Fig. VI–10b *Lift gently upward and outward to remove tape from block without stretching or curling edges.*

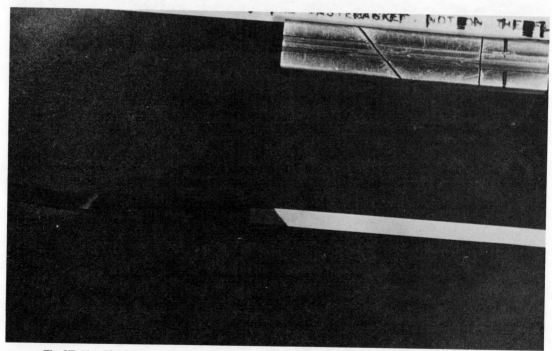

Fig. VI–11 *The finished splice; splicing tape does not overlap the edges, and the splice is free of air bubbles.*

would be to the *right* of the 45° slit and the rest of the leader to the *left* of it.

EDITING

The ability to make a good splice does not necessarily make a person a good editor. In theatre work, the majority of editing work is internal; that is, splicing the beginning of one sound directly onto the end of another, or cutting out a click or a stretch of silence, or even joining two sounds or pieces of music in the middle where there is no natural break. This takes a very good ear and, for some editing, a trained ear. You must learn to distinguish a trumpet from an oboe or the decay of one sound from the attack of another as they pass the playback head at very slow speed. And, in addition to the skill needed at the level of editor or sound engineer, there is also the artistic talent needed at the level of sound composer or designer—knowing how much silence to leave between two sounds or what short segments to snip out to make a sound humorous. These skills and talents come mostly with practice and it is difficult to explain in words what the ear should be listening for, but I shall describe certain editing procedures that are basic to the art of designing sound for the theatre.

Speech is in some ways the easiest type of sound to edit, assuming it is fairly clear and distinct when recorded. The first skill to acquire is being able to reproduce the rhythm patterns of speech with some accuracy. You will primarily be called upon to edit out a word or a blooper, or replace a phrase of a sentence with another "take" of the same phrase. You must have a feel for how rapidly the sentence was spoken in order to know how much space to leave between words. When you are replacing a word or phrase with a second take of the same word or phrase, the most accurate method is to mark the original at precisely the beginning of the sound formation of the first word of the phrase, leaving the space preceding it (between that word and the preceding word) intact. This is easier to do with words that begin with an explosive consonant such a T or P and much more difficult with words beginning with vowels or soft consonant sounds (Sh, Z), since you must be sure to edit precisely before the sound actually begins. Once you have marked that spot on the original take, place the tape on the splicing block and proceed to mark the exact same place on the second take. Once it is marked, lay it over the original in the splicing block and match the marks. Now you can either line the marks up with the cue mark on the splicing block and make your splice precisely at that point where the between-word silence ends and the word begins; or, if you feel the need for caution and you know you have a short space between words to play with, you can move the tape marks slightly to the left of the cue mark to make sure you are cutting in the silence and not in the beginning of the word. As long as the two tape marks remain aligned, you will retain the correct amount of silence. The end of the word or phrase would be edited in a similar manner, marking both the original and the second take at the end of the decay of the last word and retaining the following silence from the original. In the case of a single word, this is usually more difficult, as words tend to be slurred together whereas phrases are usually separated by the space of a breath or a punctuation mark.

Editing out a single word without replacing it with anything can be more difficult. If the words are slurred together you should edit the word out between the precise attack of that word and the precise attack of the next word so that the preceding word retains its complete decay and will seem to slur naturally into the next word. This is more difficult and will sound less natural if there has been a specific change of inflection on the word to be edited out; this will usually produce an unnatural inflection jump from the preceding word to the following word. This can sometimes be corrected by the addition of a little silence between the two words—a short break may smooth out an inflective or tonal difference. It is important, however, when you are splicing in a piece of "silence" that it be *recorded silence* with the same background noise and room ambience as the recording itself. Blank tape will not make a smooth bridge. It is always wise in any live recording session to record a minute or so of silence for this purpose.

These same problems of rhythm and spacing are encountered when editing music and are here perhaps even more critical. In addition, the editor should have some knowledge and understanding of music and should be able to read a score. You will need these skills if you are called upon to edit down the takes of a live recording session in which a musical piece is recorded. If you are fortunate, you will only have to splice at natural breaks in the music, where the biggest problem will be retaining the proper spacing. When doing a sound tape for a

production, however, you may be called upon to do some very unorthodox editing of a piece of music. The director might want the beginning of one movement of a symphony and the ending of another movement spliced together to make one cue, but you discover that the two movements are in different keys and you must find, within that symphony, the modulating chord necessary to get from one key to the other.

Editing sound effects covers such a diversity of requirements that I shall only be able to speak in general terms about basic methods. Those skills which were discussed in the preceding paragraphs will, of course, apply to editing sound effects as well as speech and music. Those effects that are realistic usually are easier to edit than abstract sounds. Quite frequently you will be concerned with a sound's envelope during the editing process. (See Chapter I.) The envelope is the shape of the sound, and it is possible to change the shape of the sound in the editing process. For example, a sound may have a very gradual build at the beginning and you may want a sharp attack instead. You can create the sharp attack by splicing the sound at the precise peak of the initial build (Fig. VI–12). Or with various splicing angles you can create a gradual attack out of a sharp one. (This follows from the fact that the amplitude of a sound is partially dependent on how much tape comes in contact with the playback head. By gradually increasing the width of recorded tape that passes the head, you will gradually increase the volume of sound, thus creating a gradual attack (Fig. VI–13). Similarly, the end of a sound can be edited for either a sharp or a gradual decay. These "custom"

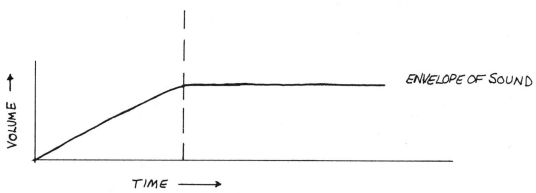

Fig. VI–12 *Creating a sharp attack on a sound that originally had a gradual attack.*

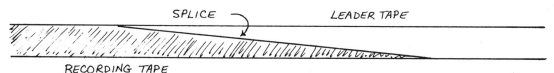

Fig. VI–13 *Creating a gradual attack on a sound that originally had a sharp attack by making a long, narrow-angle splice.*

splices are not as strong as the 45° splices and should be dubbed for final use in a show tape. Also, it must be remembered that the term "gradual" is relative. Here we are talking about the envelope of a particular sound in which a sharp attack may take 1/100th second (and be made with a 90° splice), while a gradual attack may take $\frac{1}{5}$th second (and be made with a 15° splice). We are not talking about creating gradual 4- or 5-second builds and fades in an entire sound cue by this method.

Another editing skill you should acquire for editing sound effects is that of making a tape loop. A tape loop is literally a loop of tape, the beginning spliced to the end, which has a continuous sound on it, or one sound that you wish repeated at regular intervals. You can run the loop continuously past the playback head on one machine while dubbing it

onto another. By this method you can make minutes (or even hours) of recording of a sound which was only seconds long in the original. The length of a tape loop is limited, on the short end, by how much tape it takes to circle the head-block assembly comfortably, and, on the long end, by what can fit around your studio on jerry-rigged tape guides (Fig. VI–14). Some method of maintaining tension on the loop is necessary to ensure a constant speed. With short loops this can be accomplished with a fabricated tape guide jig that can be placed on the tape deck mounting panel, or, lacking that, a round pen held steadily and firmly in the engineer's hand. For longer loops, microphone stands spaced around the loop are usually suitable. It is essential for a tape loop to have a virtually silent splice, since any extraneous noise in the cue (such as a click) will happen at a

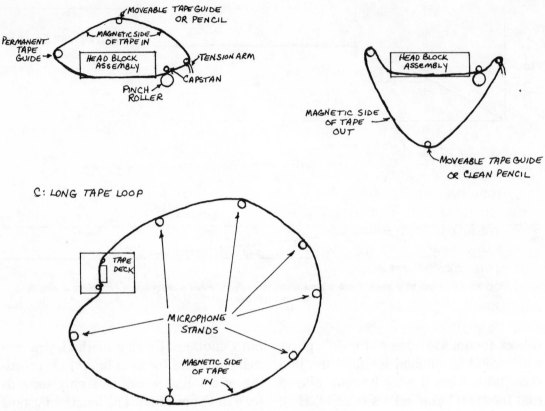

A: SHORT TAPE LOOP DONE RIGHT SIDE OUT.

B: SHORT TAPE LOOP DONE INSIDE OUT.

MOVEABLE TAPE GUIDE OR PENCIL

MAGNETIC SIDE OF TAPE IN

PERMANENT TAPE GUIDE

HEAD BLOCK ASSEMBLY

TENSION ARM

CAPSTAN

PINCH ROLLER

HEAD BLOCK ASSEMBLY

MAGNETIC SIDE OF TAPE OUT

MOVEABLE TAPE GUIDE OR CLEAN PENCIL

C: LONG TAPE LOOP

TAPE DECK

MICROPHONE STANDS

MAGNETIC SIDE OF TAPE IN

Fig. VI–14 *Various types of tape loops.*

regular interval (each time the splice passes the playback head) and will become quite noticeable and annoying. If the sound on the loop has any asymmetrical variations in it, then the shorter the loop the more obvious it will be that it is a loop.

There are virtually no rules governing the aesthetic considerations of editing sound effects. The more imaginative and creative you are, the better, and if the final product is the right sound for that particular moment in the show, it hardly matters what method you used to produce that sound. Some methods take less time than others, and that is to be encouraged; and, of course, the quality of the finished product should be as high as possible—low background noise levels; strong, silent splices; accurate editing at beginnings of cues. But how one sound connects to another within a cue, or whether a cue should begin sharply or gradually are creative choices in the hands of the show's sound designer and director.

Chapter VII

COMPOSING AND CREATING SOUND EFFECTS

Once you know the basic techniques of recording and editing, you need only to exercise your imagination in order to create sound effects. You have a show; you have met with the director and discussed the concept and the sound collage. You have done a sound plot, and now you must decide where those sounds will come from and how you will treat them to arrive at the desired final sound. As we mentioned in Chapter IV, if you are just beginning it is good to limit yourself to a certain group of sound sources and a certain style of treatment that will be effective for that show. There will, of course, be some sounds that cannot be made from the source material you have chosen, and you should not try to stretch your limited sources and style to cover absolutely every cue. The well-known expression "the exception makes the rule" also applies here.

CHOOSING THE SOURCE SOUNDS

There are five groups of source sounds. These are general headings that cover any sound that can be made. Within each group you can impose limitations if you wish. It is difficult to imagine what something will sound like from reading a description in a book, so I suggest you experiment with as many sound sources as possible and get to know the sounds they can produce.

1) *Nature Sounds and Realistic Sounds Recorded from the Actual Source.*

This is a very broad group that ranges from thunderstorms to crickets chirping and from a train braking at a crossing to someone trying to tiptoe up a creaky staircase. These sounds will often be used straight without any treatment at all. Sometimes, though, you will find that a natural or realistic sound is the best source for creating an unrealistic effect. For example, referring to the work sheet for *Macbett* in Chapter III, a typewriter was used to create a surrealistic machine-gun sound. Also, you may find you need a naturalistic sound that is out of your scope to record, so you will take a similar sound and treat it to make it sound just right. An example of that would be the sound of a large tree crashing in a forest. Although you don't happen to have a forest in your backyard, you may have a small wooded area in which there is a small dead tree no one would mind having felled. You could record the sound of the small tree falling and treat it to make it sound large and heavy.

2) *Human Sounds—Vocal and Nonvocal.*

This covers two categories: realistic "radio sound effects" and abstract, creative sounds. The first, so-called radio sounds, most people have experimented with to some degree; or at least they have seen a stand-up comedian pick up a microphone and do three minutes on "the speedway," where he does the announcer's voice, the crowds cheering, six cars zooming past (and going through four gears each), and the final crash as they all pile up on the wall in turn three. It is possible for a person to create, vocally and nonvocally, a great variety of realistic or semirealistic sounds. Thunder, creaking doors, cars starting and stopping, horses galloping and whinnying, and other animal sounds can all be created by one person with a microphone. With more than one person you can create more elaborate effects: fistfights, cattle stampeding, a whole farmyard, or a Western gun battle including runaway horses and ricocheting bullets. The radio style of sound effects is usually used only for comedy, because even when the effects are well done they are usually recognized for what they are. This can be very effective in comedy, but could prove distracting in serious drama.

Abstract human sounds, however, can be very haunting and effective in heavy drama. A subtle hint of human moans mixed with the wind can add another dimension to Strindberg or even to Shakespeare. Usually choral sounds are more effective than individual. They are most usable in productions having abstract concepts and a great deal of sound underscoring. Most often these sounds are best treated in some way or at least mixed with other sounds, but they can also be used straight. Many different source sounds are obtainable from a human chorus, and I shall mention just a few. The rest you will find through experimentation. The simplest sound to start with is a single-pitched drone—either a closed lip hum or an open AH or OH sound. To make that more interesting, split the chorus, having one group stay on that pitch and the other go a fifth higher. If you want discord, have the women on one pitch and the men one whole step down (or up) from them. Much can be done with talking or whispering. Harsh whispering (many people *not* in unison) can sound very evil and foreboding. People talking gibberish with an occasional well-chosen understandable word can key the audience to look for or expect a certain thing. In *Macbett,* one talking sequence used "Banco" as the key word. For a more abstract effect choose a consonant sound for the chorus to articulate either in or out of unison (K and T are good for this). Random screams and moans can be very useful; and heavy, raspy breathing, either unison or random, is effective. These kinds of sounds were used very effectively in a modern adaptation of Euripides' *The Bacchae* done by the Yale Repertory Theatre in 1969; the sound score was composed by Richard Peaslee.

3) *Instrumental Sounds.*

Musical instruments of all kinds are very good sources not only of music but also of sounds. Any instrument can be played as it was meant to be played and produce musical tones. These can be used either in the form of music (if the tones are organized into a musical pattern) or in the form of abstract, random tones. Most instruments can also be played in other ways than the usual to produce abstract sounds (some of which could still be considered musical). A piano, for instance, can be played by striking, rubbing, or scraping the open strings with drumsticks. The mouthpiece of a flute, particularly an electric flute, without the rest of the body, can produce interesting moans and screams. A double bass scraped with an unrosined bow is a very good source for squeaking, creaking sounds. Whistles, bells, and percussion instruments produce fine source sounds which, with a variety of treatment, run the gamut from comic to dramatic, from punctuation sounds to underscoring. With a little imagination, musical instruments are extremely useful sound sources. They can also be incorporated into a stage set and be used live in performance. If the set has metal pipe in it, holes can be cut in the pipe and instrument mouthpieces inserted; platforms can be played as drums; lightweight airplane cable and wire strung in different lengths can be plucked.

4) *Imaginative Sounds Created from What Happens to Be Near at Hand.*

This is the catch-all group of sound sources to which I turn when all else fails. It is the area that can be the most fun (and sometimes the most frustrating). Any physical object can produce a sound—strike it, blow on it, crumple it, wave it in the air—no matter what the object is, it can be made to produce a sound. Now open your ears and your imagination and really *hear* what these sounds are. Then try to imagine what

those sounds might be if they were changed somewhat. Or you can reverse the process; start with the sound you need to arrive at and think what it would sound like with variations. If it is a big, loud, reverberant sound, what would it be like on a smaller scale without the reverberation? You may find you have an object right in front of you, the sound of which, when treated properly, will be perfect. Some students of mine were creating their own "old-time radio show" and needed the sound of a whale eating an ancient Greek battleship; the solution: the sound of someone eating a potato chip, treated to sound bigger. (The treatment involved slowing the sound down, filtering it, and adding some reverberation.) Most of the time source sounds of this type do need some sort of treatment. I shall discuss various kinds of treatment later in this chapter, but for now continue to use your imagination to find other source sounds in the objects around you.

Let's go back to the sound of the tree crashing in the forest and pose the problem that you cannot get out in the woods to record even a small tree falling. You will have to create the sound in your own studio. The first step is to break down the sound into sections. First the tree creaks, then the wood cracks and splinters, then crashes through other trees on its way down, and finally hits the ground. The source for the creaking might be a double bass scraped with an unrosined bow. The wood cracking and splintering can be made by slowly breaking and tearing a piece of ¼-inch plywood. As the tree crashes through the branches of other trees you might mix the sound of twigs snapping with paper rustling. And for the final crash, the sound of a large, heavy item falling into the leftover debris (plywood, twigs, paper). All these sounds would, of course, have to be treated and properly mixed to get the right amount of overlapping of the different sounds, but if properly done it could be a very effective sound.

Many sounds can be created this way. Crisp paper being crumpled is a good source for fire. Mix it with some cracking wood and crashing sounds and you have a house burning down. A large sheet of mylar foil held at opposite ends by two people and waved through the air is the basis for a seashore (waves and breakers). Abstract sounds are virtually unlimited from this source—bottles, pots and pans, stones rolling around in a large pot or in a wooden box, water being poured or splashed or dripped, a fork scraped across a piece of sheet metal. Use your imagination and see what you come up with.

5) *Pure Sounds (Wave Forms) from Generators.*

If your studio has some wave form or signal generators, these can be good sources for a limited amount of sounds. (Sine and square wave and white noise generators are the most commonly found.) These are always good for short-wave radio cues (the sound of scanning the frequencies before being tuned in) and with a little imagination can be used to create fictional computer beeps and buzzes for science-fiction plays. They can also be used to create harmonic tones to be mixed with other sounds to produce interesting effects. If your studio is fortunate enough to have these generators in the form of an electronic synthesizer, then the possibilities for sound creation

are limited only by time, patience, and imagination. An elaborate explanation of synthesizers is beyond the scope of this book, but suffice it to say that such an instrument can be an unending source of interesting sounds. It can also become a source of very boring sounds if it is overused in making showtapes. A better use of the synthesizer in a theatre sound studio is as a sound *treatment* unit rather than as a sound *source* unit.

Treatment of Sounds

The basic techniques of treating sounds were discussed in Chapter V. When to use these techniques and what the result will be is the subject for this chapter. These techniques can be used individually or in combination and, once again, experimentation is the best teacher of what will work.

1) *Speed Distortion.*

With a continuously variable speed tape deck, small increments of speed change are possible for use in slightly altering the pitch or tempo of music or speech. A small speed change may not be noticeable as distortion but may accomplish the pitch or tempo change you desire. For example, an actor may do a voiceover and the director might decide that the voice should be a little lower pitched for the characterization he wants. By slowing the cue down 4 or 5 percent, you can achieve the pitch change without having the speech become too distorted. Or if a piece of music must time exactly to a speech it is meant to underscore and the one-minute piece of music is three seconds too long, it could be speeded up by 5 percent. It would then time out right, and only a critical musician might notice the

Composing and Creating Sound Effects / 103

change. These are the simplest uses of speed change.

On a broader scale, sounds can be considerably altered and distorted by speed change. By making a sound considerably slower, you can make it sound much bigger. This is because as the speed becomes slower, the pitch or frequency becomes lower. (For a fuller explanation, see Chapter I.) If you have the sound of a pistol shot but need the sound of a large rifle, slow the pistol shot to half speed. If you need the sound of church bells chiming the hour but all you have is a hand chime or the sound of a mantel clock chiming, slow your sound down to half or even quarter speed. A small splash will sound like a large body falling into water at half speed, and a small wooden door can be made to sound like a great oaken door. In reverse, a large sound can be made to sound smaller by speeding it up. Although this is not quite so common in making realistic sounds, it is very useful in abstract sounds.

2) Mixing.

Mixing is usually thought of in terms of two or more sounds that go together harmoniously to create a more complex effect, such as mixing wind, rain, and thunder to create a storm. Mixing is also useful, in combination with other treatment techniques, in changing an existing sound. If a particular sound is too thin and needs to be fuller, richer, or deeper, make a dub of the sound at half speed, then mix the two together. This trick will work even for some kinds of music; the half-speed dub will be in the same key as the original but down one octave, so it will be harmonious with the original and will add a deep, rich bass line. Needless to say, this method cannot be used on a

well-known piece of music and does not work as well on a highly melodic piece as on a nonmelodic piece. On a more abstract level, sounds can be mixed with other sounds that are not so harmonious to create intentional distortion effects. Any two single tones that are very close but not identical in frequency will, when mixed, undergo partial reinforcement and cancellation in a regular pattern. This is heard as "beats," a kind of throbbing effect. This and other psychoacoustic phenomena will be explained more thoroughly in Chapter IX.

3) Reverse Direction.

Reversing the direction of a sound is usually used for abstract effects. The most notable result of playing a sound backward is that the envelope or shape of the sound is reversed. That is, a sound which has a sharp attack and a long decay will, in reverse, have a long gradual attack and a sudden ending that may sound like a blip. This change in shape can be very effective in creating odd versions of sounds that you still wish to be recognizable; a bell or other musical tone is very adaptable to this, although you may wish to do a fast fade-out at the end to avoid the blip that was the initial strike. A show that has supernatural beings or influences can make use of the reverse-direction technique for music and speech as well as sounds. The one drawback to this technique is that it is very recognizable for what it is, and it should be disguised whenever possible. Sounds are usually more effective when your tricks and methods are not obvious for the audience to hear.

4) Filtering.

The filter or equalizer is one of the most useful pieces of equipment in the studio. Both by itself and in combination with other techniques, filtering can accomplish a wide variety of alterations to sound effects. The most obvious use of the filter is to remove scratch and hiss and other unwanted noise from old and/or bad recordings. You can also add hiss and noise to good recordings to make them sound old. This is done by boosting both the extreme high and low frequencies and attenuating the next band in at either end (Fig. VII–1). This

to achieve certain effects. Low frequencies, because their wavelengths are longer than high frequencies, travel farther before dissipating. A distant sound, therefore, contains mostly lower frequencies and possibly some mid-range (Fig. VII–2). The same is true of a sound traveling through a wall or other barrier. The barrier is more acoustically transparent to lower frequencies, whereas it readily absorbs high frequencies. If you are going to add reverberation to a sound to

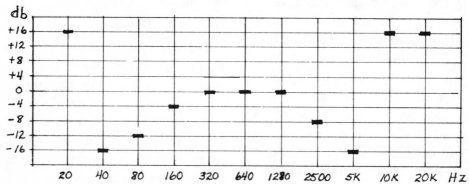

Fig. VII–1 *Equalizer settings for making a new record sound old. (These settings are suggestions. The student is advised to experiment to find precisely the right sound for his particular need.)*

will emphasize any scratch, hiss, and noise already in the recording but limit the frequency range of the sound or music (a characteristic of old recordings). In a complex mix of sounds or music, it may be possible to boost or deemphasize one particular sound or instrument if you can find the frequency band in which lies either the fundamental or the dominant harmonic of that sound or instrument. You may at the same time be boosting or attenuating some other sound or instrument, depending on the nature of the complex sound. This can only be determined by experimentation in each particular case.

Certain facts of acoustics will aid you in determining the proper filter settings

effect a large, hollow chamber, you might also filter the sound to emphasize certain mid-range or lower mid-range frequencies. Most reverberant rooms have a resonant frequency in the lower mid-range. You can make a voice or sound very hollow by attenuating the mid-range and boosting the low and high frequencies; or make it mellow by boosting the mid-range somewhat. So some experimenting is necessary with each sound you wish to change.

In combination with other techniques, filtering can be used to create more complex effects. If you have a stereo filter (with separate controls for each channel) and a continuously variable speed tape deck, you can create the Dopler effect

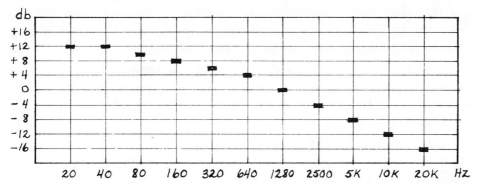

Fig. VII–2 *Equalizer settings to affect distance. (These settings are suggestions. The student is advised to experiment to find precisely the right sound for his particular need.)*

(the way the sound of a train changes as it approaches, passes by, and disappears). Set up your filter as in Fig. VII–3. Put the tape of the sound to be changed on the variable speed deck. (It should be a two-track recording with the same sound on both tracks.) Put one track through Channel I of the filter and the other through Channel II. Start the deck at a slow speed (maybe 15 or 20 percent slower than normal), with the volume up for Channel I only. Slowly bring the

speed up to normal and at the same time (and same rate) crossfade from Channel I to Channel II. Then reduce the speed of the tape while crossfading back to Channel I.

5) *Reverberation and Echo Effects.*

Reverberation can be added to a dead recording to create the effect of natural room ambience. This makes the recording rich and dimensional. Not much reverberation is necessary to effect ambi-

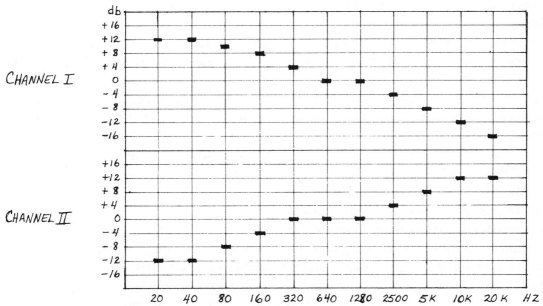

Fig. VII–3 *Equalizer settings to create Dopler effect. (These settings are suggestions. The student is advised to experiment to find precisely the right sound for his particular needs.)*

ence in a recording, and when using a spring reverberation unit as opposed to the plate type, care should be used that the reverberation does not become excessive. Reverberation or echo can also be used to make a sound hollow or distant or bigger. (This is usually done in combination with filtering or a speed change.) Experimentation is the best guide to how much reverberation is necessary for a particular cue. For some sounds a tape-delay type echo is more effective than a reverberation unit. For example, the sound of water dripping inside a cave would probably be better with echo rather than reverberation, whereas many abstract, "weird" sounds are better with a spring reverberation treatment. The spring reverberation unit is very effective for creating supernatural and eerie sounds, but, of course, the overuse of this treatment will dull its effectiveness. The supernatural type of sound effects made electronically (with a synthesizer) have, unfortunately, become cliché, and any effects that sound electronic (which a heavy amount of reverberation will cause) are put in that category and dismissed as "hokie electronic sound." This is not to say that reverberation effects and even purely electronic sounds cannot be used, but they must be used carefully and with a light hand lest they do indeed become cliché.

6) *Phase Distortion.*

This phenomenon is a particularly useful treatment technique. With various amounts of phase distortion, a sound can remain recognizable while being very different in quality from the original. At the same time, the method of treatment is not so recognizable. Therefore this method of treatment becomes a viable

alternative to such easily recognized techniques as reverse direction and reverberation. Phase distortion can, of course, be used in combination with other treatments, particularly the filter, which will help vary the amount of phase distortion if the two channels are filtered differently. (See Chapter V for complete explanation of how this is done.)

7) *Ring Modulation.*

The ring modulator is another device that will change sounds in an uncommon and unrecognizable manner. In this case, however, the original sound may also be unrecognizable, depending on what sound it was modulated against. Since the function of the ring modulator is dependent on two separate input signals, it is impossible to describe how one particular sound will end up after this treatment. The device is excellent for completely changing a piece of music—simply modulate the music against a single tone (sine or square wave). Try it out on sounds, too, first modulating a sound against a single tone, then against a sweeping tone (one that changes frequency), then against another sound. My only advice for using this technique is to record the results the first time you try any two inputs, because you may never be able to achieve the same results twice (since a slight difference of frequency or timing would change the resultant sound).

SETTING LEVELS IN THE THEATRE

A very important part of designing sound effects is determining how they will be played back in the theatre. The effect of any one sound can be completely different depending on what speakers it is playing through, how loud it is played, and whether it fades in and out or is punched on. Speaker determination is often based on realistic directionality of a sound—the car honk comes from stage left because that is where the open window is, the piano music comes from up stage right because that is where the other room is, etc. With some sounds, mostly environmental ones such as storms, street noises, or crickets, you have the choice of whether to include the audience in the environment or leave the sound strictly on stage. This is usually the director's decision, but sometimes a director will need to be reminded that he can play a sound through the house speakers. With abstract sounds and underscoring for "concept" productions, the audience is almost always included, and sounds will often bounce from one speaker to another around the house. If your tape is in stereo, you have the choice of doing either left and right stereo or front and rear stereo. In an arena theatre, strict directionality is difficult to achieve, but there is still the choice of having the sound radiate from the stage outward or from the back of the audience inward.

Determining the proper playback level of a cue can be very difficult. Realistic cues that happen in the clear (that is, not under dialogue) can usually be played at what would be a realistic level. Sometimes a director will wish to make a point by playing a sound much louder (or even much softer) than would be realistic. This can be done either for comic effect or to build tension. When a sound is underscoring dialogue, it is sometimes effective to have it playing at a subliminal level, almost below the level of conscious awareness, so that it is a feeling more

than a sound. I used this level for the wind under the Margaret–Bertha scene in Strindberg's *The Father;* the audience did not really hear the wind, but they felt a chill. Very loud levels can also be effective for brief periods of time, but continual bombardment with loud sounds can put an audience in a very bad frame of mind (to say nothing of giving them a headache), which will dull the effectiveness of the production for them.

One of the trickiest aspects of setting sound levels is that for a long-run production the "correct" levels may change considerably depending on how a show grows and what the actors do differently during the course of the run. When a show opens, an actor may be doing a speech very intensely but very intimately (that is, with not very much volume). If there is a sound or music cue underscoring that speech, it would have to be at a low level. But if the actor gradually becomes bolder with the speech and begins to deliver it with great energy and increased volume, then the sound cue, in order to remain effective, may also have to be increased in volume. Even cues that are not underscoring but are out in the clear may lose some of their effectiveness if they remain at the original levels while the energy of the actors and the pace of the show pick up. On the opposite side of the coin, I would not necessarily lower the levels of any cues on a night when the actors start out a little lacking in energy. A very tightly run and energetic physical performance can sometimes pick up sluggish actors and bring a show up to its proper energy level. (Psychology is just as useful on the performers and running crew as it is on the audience.)

Chapter VIII

MUSIC IN THE THEATRE

CHOOSING A MUSICAL STYLE

Incidental music for a theatrical production should be as closely related to the director's production concept as the set, costumes, lighting, and sound. At an early stage of the planning, the director, together with the composer—if there is one—and the person doing sound, must decide whether music will be used at all, and, if it is used, where it will occur and what kind of music it will be.

Deciding what kind of music to use is exactly like deciding on a sound collage. Various elements in the production concept should suggest an overall musical sound: a kind of tempo, rhythm, style, and instrumentation. Here the advice of a musician can be especially helpful, because the director and the sound specialist may not be familiar with a wide enough variety of music to know all the choices that are available.

The choice of a musical style can go a long way toward giving a production the particular tone that the director may want. A domestic drama with a Victorian setting might use piano music of the kind that was played in Victorian households. *Hamlet,* in one kind of production, might need music with an archaic quality, to emphasize the medieval barbarity of Elsinore castle and what goes on there. An-

other kind of production might have an electronic score, because the director wants to convey a contemporary impression of Hamlet's alienation. Music for *The Tempest* requires very careful thought. Suppose the director has decided to set the production in the 1890's. The shipwrecked people are dressed in period costumes, and, perhaps, characterized by period music. When they hear the music of the island, is it the kind of magical music a 19th-century composer would have imagined; that is, something not entirely outside the characters' experience? Or is it something completely new and unfamiliar? The answer depends on how the director interprets the play.

Period music is not always appropriate, of course, and sometimes it has to be avoided. I once had to decide not to use real French vaudeville music of the 1900's for a Feydeau play in which the leading character is a music-hall singer, because to a modern audience it sounds old-fashioned and certainly does not have the kind of sparkle and excitement the music for a farce ought to have. Instead I used the more familiar sound of ragtime and circus music, which I thought would give the audience the right feeling, even if the period and place were wrong.

Sometimes a script specifies particular

music. Strindberg, for example, wants one of Chopin's *Nocturnes* to be played throughout the last scene of *The Great Highway*. In such cases, it may not always be right to follow the playwright's directions. The director may have a different idea of the play, or the music called for in the script may not have the same effect now as it did when the play was written.

USING MUSIC IN A DRAMATIC PRODUCTION

After the musical style of a production has been set, it is important to decide very carefully where in the play the music is to be used. This choice, like the choice of a musical style, must always be made with reference to the overall concept of the show.

These are some of the ways in which music is most commonly used:

1) Preshow music.
2) Music used during set changes.
3) Music, such as the music of a passing parade, that the script says is heard by the characters on stage.
4) Standard musical effects, such as fanfares for the entrances of kings and their courts in Shakespeare.
5) Accompaniment for pantomimes and dumb shows.
6) Songs and dances.
7) Music that is used to introduce or close an act or a scene (if music is used at the beginning and the end, the arrangement is called "framing").
8) Music that underscores action or dialogue.

Of these ways of using music, only underscoring presents special problems. Review the remarks in Chapter IV about underscoring with sound. They apply just as well to music. In general, music used for underscoring should not call attention to itself. It should be free of distracting changes of tempo, mood, texture, or volume, *especially when it accompanies dialogue.* But it must not be too monotonous: monotony itself can prove distracting. It should strike a balance between consistency and variety, leaning strongly toward the side of consistency. As a rule, music that succeeds in doing this has details that keep changing, even in small ways that the audience does not notice consciously, while the overall texture stays the same.

When the scene that it accompanies is over, musical underscoring as a rule fades out unobtrusively. Strictly on musical grounds, it might be better if the music could come to some kind of conclusion instead of fading out, but that is not practical. The pace of performances varies too much for anyone to know exactly how long a piece of background music would have to be. If it is absolutely necessary to have musical underscoring that changes with the mood and pace of the action on stage, the music must be given to the actors early in the rehearsal period, and they must rehearse with it until they learn to follow it. It is a mistake to think that any piece of music is strong enough to lead actors in its path without rehearsal. In performance they are likely to become absorbed in their acting and ignore the music.

The places in a production where music is used inevitably are set apart from the rest of the play, and they may well come across with more emphasis, especially if the music is very strong. This is the main point that director, composer, and sound specialist must keep in mind when they decide where they want music to be used. As a rule, scenes should be underscored only when there is a good reason for stressing them. The choice of scenes to be stressed should always reflect an interpretation of the play. For example, to use music in *Macbeth* during the scene where the murder of Duncan is discovered underlines for the audience the enormity of Macbeth's crime. But if music is used instead to underscore the soliloquy before the murder, then Macbeth's character is made to seem more important than what he does. The more routine uses of music should be scaled according to their dramatic importance. Fanfares may be short or long, depending on how strongly the director wants to set up the scene that follows. Songs that are incidental to the action of the play should be brief and casual. But songs that occur at vital dramatic moments (such as Grusha's song on the bridge in *The Caucasian Chalk Circle*) need more elaborate musical settings.

Sometimes music can be used with a dramatic meaning that remains consistent throughout a production. In a production of a farce with a chase sequence in each act, I used music to underscore only the chases. The same music was used each time, of course, and it returned at the end for the curtain calls, tying the show together to the great satisfaction of the audience. (There also was music at the beginning of each act. It served to establish the presence of music in the production, so that the underscoring of the chase scenes did not come as an un-

settling surprise.) In a more serious play, a single musical theme might be used throughout, either changing each time it appeared to reflect the development of the drama, or remaining the same to indicate an obsession, or a situation that does not change. A production of *Hamlet* that I worked on was made very stark and bleak, in part because music was used only when it occurred as a natural part of the stage action, during the dumb show (it was played live on stage by actors in the Players' entourage), when Fortinbras' army crosses the stage, and when Ophelia and the Gravedigger sing. Their songs were completely unaccompanied. The production was given a kind of large-scale form by a combination of music and sound. The first act was framed by wordless muttering of the Ghost's voice at the beginning, and the rather brutal music of Fortinbras' army at the end. A sound effect brought the production to a close at the end of the second act, too, but it was very simple: a few cannon shots, mentioned in the last line of the text. In terms of sound, the ending was rather bleak and uncompromising. The words and actions were allowed to speak for themselves. In contrast to this, if music had been used to underscore Hamlet's death, the effect would have been sentimental. The music would have seemed like a commentary on the action, as if the audience were being told how to feel.

Generally speaking, incidental music is most effective when very little of it is used. If there are many musical cues, they must be carefully varied and paced, or the music will lose its effect because it has become too predictable. It is much more difficult to be successful using a lot of music than it is to be successful using a little. Often no more is needed than a few moments at the beginning to bring the curtain up and establish a mood.

PRACTICAL ASPECTS OF MUSIC IN THE THEATRE

1) *Using Preexisting Music.*

Once the decisions have been made about the musical style to be used and the places where the cues will come, it is time to proceed to the actual music. If original music is needed, there will have to be a composer to write it. If there is no composer, and the theatre has no musical director, the person doing sound usually has the job of finding suitable music on records to put on tape and use for the show. Sometimes, of course, the director will specify the music to be used.

The disadvantages of using preexisting music were mentioned in Chapter IV. The advantages are obvious, the main one, of course, being that the music already exists and is there to be taken, without much work needed to appropriate it. For this reason, preexisting music is very often used. Obviously, the more the person who chooses the music knows about music in general, the better. Two words of warning:

a) It is not a good idea to use music that is too well known (such as Beethoven's 5th Symphony, or the *1812 Overture*) because it carries with it associations that have nothing to do with the play. In fact, if the music is so familiar that it has become a kind of cliché, it may strike the audience as a comment on the play and may even make the play seem like a parody of itself. Stanley Kubrick used *The Blue Danube* waltz in this way on purpose in the scene in *2001* where the shuttle docks at the space station. It is important to avoid creating the same effect by accident.

b) It is not a good idea to use music which in its original form is associated with a dramatic meaning of its own, even if most of the audience will not recognize it. The better such music is, the less suitable it is to use on stage. Some people *will* recognize it, and they may feel that something they love has been torn out of its proper place. The production may be ruined for them.

2) *Using Live Music.*

Live music adds a definite touch of class to any show. It is in itself rather theatrical and brightens performances where it is used. There may be other reasons for using it, too. Sometimes the script or the production concept requires musicians to play on stage as part of the action. If a show has songs, it is always better to have the accompaniments played live, so that the actors are not tied to a taped accompaniment that cannot change with the mood or pace of a particular performance. But if the songs are at all complicated musically, there is no choice. The accompaniments *must* be live, or there is no way of assuring that they can truly accompany the singing.

Live music, however, has problems all its own. The obvious one is that musicians must be found and, very likely, paid. But it is the less obvious problems that always cause trouble. These are some points to watch for—and, small as many of them may seem, every one has brought me grief in some production:

a) If there are instrumentalists playing

from written music, they will need music stands, and, in all probability, stand lights. It is not unreasonable to ask instrumentalists to bring their own stands; they all have them. But they must be told in advance. The best music-stand light is the standard orchestral kind that clips onto the back of the stand. They are fairly expensive to buy but can usually be borrowed from a college or university music department. However, they are too heavy to use with the thin wire music stands that instrumental players usually have, so if you borrow music-stand lights you will also need to borrow the heavy metal music stands that professional orchestras use. If stand lights cannot be borrowed, they can be built, or jerry-rigged from clip-on lamps that can be bought at most hardware stores. *But that is not as easy to do as it seems!* More than once I have seen musicians rather angrily dismantle the improvised stand lights that the technical staff of a production were sure would be all right. The job should not be left to the last minute, and it should be done in close consultation with the musicians or the conductor. Two final points about lights and stands. If the glare from the lights is visible to the audience, as it often is when there is no orchestra pit, the problem can be solved with colored gels. And if, as occasionally happens, the musicians are on stage, and their stands are built into the set, the height of the stands must be made adjustable. It is not enough to build the stands so that they are comfortable for the people who are scheduled to play the entire run of the show. It is very likely that there will

be substitutes in some of the performances, and more likely the more professional the musicians are.

b) The actors must be able to see the conductor, if there is one. Ideally the conductor should be able to see the faces of the actors when they sing; then they will have maximum freedom, because the conductor will be able to anticipate what they are about to do, and can follow them. Directors, however, often want to put the conductor and the instruments backstage, off to the side, or on stage in back of the actors, all for the sake of a pretty stage picture. Unfortunately, when conductor and singers are completely out of contact with each other, disaster may strike at any moment. If the conductor *must* be put in some spot that the actors cannot see, they ought to be given the beat on closed-circuit TV. The camera is attached somewhere where it will pick up the conductor's beat, and a monitor is put out in the house where the actors can see it, perhaps at the front of the balcony, if there is one. This may sound like an extravagant suggestion, but experience has proved it to be both necessary and practical. University theatres, at least, should have easy access to closed-circuit TV equipment through the audiovisual department. If the conductor is in the usual place, in front of the stage and facing the actors, the set designer and the director must make sure that every actor who needs to see the beat will be able to see it. In particular, the set designer should make sure that the beat is visible from all upstage platforms and risers, no matter how many people may be in the way downstage—bearing in mind that a conductor's beat is usually chest-high.

3) *Using Original Music.*

An original score for a dramatic production is, in a way, the result of a collaboration between the director and the composer. The composer is, in the last analysis, helping to carry out the director's concept of the play; he must understand that the director has the final say on what the music will be. The director, in turn, should recognize that the composer is a specialist whose ideas about how music might be used are worth careful attention. The relationship is sometimes an uneasy one. The composer is often an outsider in the theatre world, and the director, who probably is not a trained musician, may find it hard to understand the composer's descriptions of the kinds of music it might be possible to use. (Music is very hard to describe without using technical language.) The collaboration works best when neither party has fixed ideas, when both are willing to work out a plan for the music together. Once the general concept has been set, the composer should be given complete freedom to realize it in detail, subject, of course, to the director's approval of the final result.

Music cues have a way of changing during the rehearsal period of a show. They are rarely set in final form until the dress rehearsal—and sometimes not even then. Composer and director must both be aware that, beyond a certain time— which may come sooner than everybody expects—major changes in the music will not be possible. If the music is to be performed live, it usually is added to the show at the first dress rehearsal (not at the tech rehearsal, because instrumentalists cannot be expected to sit around for hours with only a few minutes of playing to do). The composer must have finished writing it early enough before the dress rehearsal to have time to orchestrate it, copy the parts, and rehearse the players (bearing in mind that rehearsals will have to be planned around the instrumentalists' schedules, and may not be able to be as late as the composer might like). Once the music is set, changes are possible only within certain limits. Cuts are easy to make, but new cues can be added only if the ensemble has time to learn them. A good rule of thumb: new cues are safe only if the players are able to sight-read them. Anything requiring extensive rehearsal is out of the question.

The situation is worse if the music is to be taped. Taped music is added to the show at the tech rehearsal, which of course is earlier than the dress rehearsal. So the composer must have the music finished earlier; actually, quite a bit earlier because, apart from the usual orchestrating, copying, and rehearsing, extra time must be allowed for a recording session, and for editing the tapes. (It is best to set aside a full day for editing the tapes.) Music that is going to be taped must be written at least a week before the tech rehearsal. Put another way, taped music for a show with a three-week rehearsal period may have to be set when the rehearsals are only half over. Composer and director cannot afford the time to discover what they want to do during the rehearsals.

Once the music has been taped, some small changes are possible. The music on the tape can be cut, by splicing the tape. It can be lengthened, by making a copy of the tape and splicing in a repetition of something that is already there. The composer should bear these possibilities in mind from the start and if possible write music that will make it easy to take advantage of them. Whenever there is any doubt about how much music is needed for a given cue, more should be written than seems necessary, because it is easier to cut music than to add it. Music that may have to be shortened or lengthened should be written so that it breaks up easily into many short sections. If it is skillfully done, the audience and the actors will not hear the sectional divisions, but they will be there all the same to provide innumerable joints at which material may be cut or added.

Chapter IX

PSYCHOACOUSTICS

The field of psychoacoustics is relatively new, and although many experiments have been made, there are still some unexplained phenomena. The results of many psychoacoustical experiments must be read with some caution, since they are based on subjective data rather than objective, scientifically measurable data. In an experiment to determine the relative loudness (subjectively) of tones of different amplitudes, we take data on when a person *thinks* one tone is twice as loud as another. It is not within the scope of this book to delve into the experiments in this field or to try to explain the often strange results. Rather it is the purpose of this chapter to explore the importance of these results in terms of composing sound and music for the theatre. The student who wishes to learn more about the experiments and the explanation of the results is referred to the books listed in the bibliography.

SUBJECTIVE RESPONSES TO SOUND

Objectively, sound is measured in terms of amplitude or intensity, frequency, wave form, and envelope. Subjectively, these are measured in terms of loudness, pitch, timbre, and duration. Let us examine these one at a time. The ear is most sensitive to sound at approximately 3000 Hz. That is where hearing is most acute in the normal, healthy person. On both sides of 3000 Hz hearing becomes gradually less acute, so that a sound of lower frequency, say 400 Hz, will have to be of greater intensity to be heard at the same loudness as the 3000-Hz tone. The intensity at which a sound is just barely audible is called the threshold of hearing. This threshold varies considerably with frequency. As overall intensity is increased, it eventually produces a tickling sensation in the ear at approximately 120 db. This is known as the threshold of feeling, and this threshold varies very little with frequency (Fig. IX–1). This would indicate that the relative loudness of sounds of different fre-

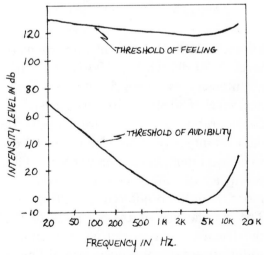

Fig. IX–1 *Thresholds of audibility and feeling in decibels (0db = 10⁻¹² watts/M²). (After Kinsler and Frey.)*

quencies but the same intensity varies as the overall intensity changes. Unfortunately for the sound engineer, this is indeed true.

Loudness is measured in units called phons, and the measurement is based on the *intensity* level in db of a 1000-Hz tone. That is, the loudness level in phons of any tone is numerically equal to the intensity level in db (with reference to 10^{-12}w/m^2) of a 1000-Hz tone of equal loudness. The loudness curve is shown in Figure IX–2. For a loudness level of 20

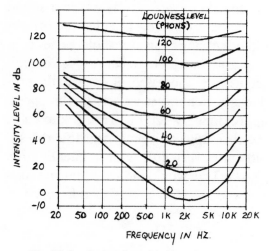

Fig. IX–2 *Curves of equal loudness level (0db = 10^{-12} W/M^2).* (After Kinsler and Frey.)

phons, a 1000-Hz tone has an intensity level of 20 db, while a 100-Hz tone has an intensity level over 50 db. At a loudness level of 80 phons the curve levels out considerably: a 100-Hz tone needs to have an intensity of approximately 83 db to have a loudness level of 80 phons. This is only a 3-db difference as opposed to the more than 30-db difference at 20 phons. The significance of these curves to the theatrical sound designer is great. In any sound or piece of music containing a broad range of frequencies, the loudness

relationship of the component frequencies will change as the overall intensity is changed. If the sound is played at an intensity level of 20 db, frequencies below approximately 300 Hz will not even be heard and the frequencies between 300 Hz and 1000 Hz will not sound as loud as the higher frequencies. (It is for this reason that there is a loudness compensation switch on many commercial preamplifiers that will boost the bass frequencies according to the loudness curve. This switch should be engaged only when the output volume is at a low level, and, to be absolutely correct, it should include some very high frequency boost as well as low frequency.) If the same sound is played at an intensity level of 80 db, the whole range of frequencies will be heard at almost the same loudness level. It is this change in balance among the frequencies that makes it essential to record sounds or music at the same level at which they will be played back in the theatre. As an example, suppose orchestral music is to be recorded for a show (played by an orchestra in a live recording session, not to be dubbed off records). The orchestra should play each cue at the level at which it is to be heard in performance so that the conductor can balance the instruments according to that level. If a cue is played by the orchestra at 90 db but then played back in the theatre at 30 db, such instruments as the double bass will hardly come through at all, whereas they might have been in perfect balance while the orchestra was playing the cue. If the cue had been played softly to begin with and the instruments had been blended correctly at that level, then the cue would sound as it should when played back at that level.

The chart in Figure IX–3 shows essentially the reverse of the loudness curves. Here we see the loudness level in phons of the different frequencies of a given intensity. In other words, if the intensity level is 40 db, a 1000-Hz tone will have a loudness level of 40 phons while a 200-Hz tone will have a loudness level of only 20 phons and a 50-Hz tone will be heard by only the best of us. These charts are meant for general guidance on the subject of loudness versus intensity. They should not be held as absolute fact when applied to sound and music cues, because the charts were compiled from data collected using individual pure sine tones. The data would change somewhat for complex waves containing a broad range of frequencies. However, the charts do remain useful as guides to the principles of how loudness levels differ from intensity levels according to frequency and overall intensity.

There is one other important area in which we should learn from the loudness curves. When you are in the studio using equipment that is capable of generating very low frequency sounds (especially pure sine tones), be careful not to turn the gain up loud. You won't be able to hear the sound very well if it is below 25 or 30 Hz, and the temptation will be to turn the gain up in order to hear it better. But in turning up the volume you could destroy the speakers with a sound which to you is not very loud but which in actual intensity level is enough to drive the speaker cone past its excursion limit. The same is true at the very high end of the frequency range. Most tweeters are not built to sustain long periods of high frequencies at high intensities, although they can handle the instantaneous peaks and bursts that are found in music. When experimenting with very high frequency pure tones, once again the temptation may be to turn up the gain in order to compensate for the lower sensitivity of the ear at those frequencies. Don't give in to that temptation unless you have adequate fuse protection in your speaker circuits.

The pitch of a tone is primarily dependent upon its frequency, although experiments have shown that subjective pitch is not necessarily related to musical

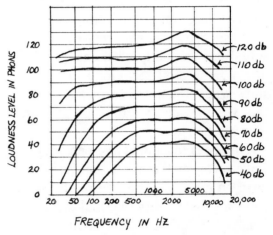

Fig. IX–3 *Curves of equal intensity expressed in phons.*

pitch. The subjective unit of pitch is known as a *mel*. The mel was arrived at by assigning to a 1000-Hz tone a subjective pitch of 1000 mels. The tone that is subjectively half that pitch is said to be 500 mels. If there were a musical correspondence, this would occur at 500 Hz, which is half the frequency of a 1000-Hz tone and one octave below it. Unfortunately, the tone having a subjective pitch of 500 mels is just under 400 Hz. It may be for this reason that "perfect pitch," musically, is so rare and is usually acquired through training. In fact, except in those cases where a person has perfect pitch, exact memory of pitch (or loudness or timbre, for that matter) cannot be retained over any length of time. This applies, of course, to single, unrelated tones; melodic structure is fairly easily retained in the memory. But the sound designer should keep this in mind when attempting to make a point through subtle differences in sound: the longer the time span, the less subtle can be the differences between two sounds if they are to be recognized as different. Over a period of time, however, a *series* of subtle changes may be effective; the initial changes may not be noticed, but eventually the audience will realize that the sound has gradually been changed. This might be a good technique to use in a show where the mood shifts gradually or the villain's deeds grow progressively more evil.

Timbre is the subjective perception of wave form, or the effect that harmonics have on a sound. The timbre of a sound is the distinct quality that makes it distinguishable from another sound of the same pitch and loudness. (It is what enables one to distinguish between a violin and an oboe even though both are playing the same note.) Timbre is not solely a function of wave form but also of intensity and frequency in the form of distortion. Distortion can take place in one of three areas: physically or electronically within the sound producer, acoustically within the environment through which the sound passes to reach the ears, and psychoacoustically within the hearing mechanism itself. The last of these is very difficult to quantify, but it has been established that when two tones of different frequency are sounded simultaneously at a fairly high intensity, a person will perceive not only the two initial tones but also their sum and difference frequencies if they are within the audible range. To a great extent we hear what we are trained to hear and what we want to hear. A person can grow accustomed to a certain amount of sound distortion and not even realize that the sound is distorted. And a person can believe one sound to be a good imitation of another if he listens to it repeatedly and if that is the result he wants. This is a particular danger to the sound designer, who spends so many hours in the studio that he becomes deaf to the imperfections of the sounds he is creating. It is always best to hear your sounds with a fresh perspective.

The last of the subjective responses to sound is duration. This seems fairly straightforward: We hear a sound at a certain loudness for as long as it is sustained at that intensity, then we hear it die out for as long as it or its reverberations remain above the threshold of hearing. This is more or less true, but there are some peculiarities about the hearing mechanism that break this rule. For instance, we do not perceive a sound at its maximum loudness level instantly. It takes somewhere in the neighborhood of 0.3 second for a sound to attain its maximum loudness level (assuming its intensity level is unchanged). For a sound of long duration and unchanging intensity level, the loudness level will remain at its maximum for several seconds, then decrease steadily. The curves in Figure IX–4 show this effect at various intensities. Particularly in the case of high intensity sounds, the ear will accustom itself to and sometimes protect itself from

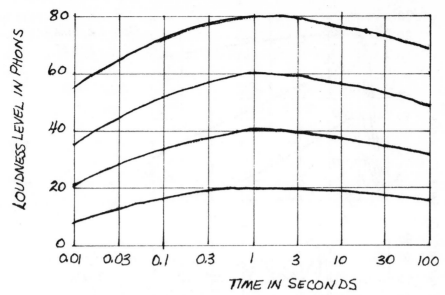

Fig. IX–4   *Relation of loudness level to duration (after Munson).*

that intensity by damping the sound somewhat. This is known as *auditory adaptation*. This should be remembered when setting levels; the effectiveness of a loud sound will diminish with time. That is not to suggest that you damage everyone's hearing by steadily increasing levels of a long-duration cue, but merely to point out that the effectiveness of high-intensity levels can be limited.

It is also a peculiarity of the hearing mechanism or perhaps of the brain that, particularly with high-intensity sounds, we may continue to "hear" a sound for a short time after it has stopped. This concerns us only in that it may take an audience a second or two to regain aural concentration on an actor after a particularly loud sound cue.

MASKING AND AUDITORY FATIGUE

We have all experienced the phenomenon that when a very loud background noise is present we cannot hear specific desired sounds. For instance, when you are driving down a highway and a large tractor-trailer truck roars by, the sound of a person talking is completely drowned out. This is known as masking, when the presence of one sound requires that the intensity of another sound be raised above its normal threshold in order to be just barely audible. Although most commonly we are concerned with masking by "noise" (sound covering a wide band of all or indiscriminate frequencies), we can learn a great deal about masking by studying experiments in masking with pure tones. A pure tone generally produces a greater masking effect on frequencies very close to those of the masking tone and its harmonics. The curves in Figure IX–5 show typical masking patterns for pure tones. The vertical axis indicates the rise in threshold of the signal tone for it to be just audible in the presence of the masking tone. The horizontal axis indicates frequency of the signal tone, and the decibel figure for

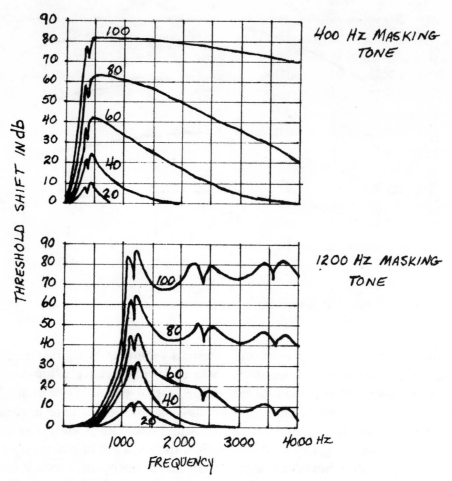

Fig. IX–5 *Masking curves; number above curve indicates intensity of masking tone* (after van Bergeijk, Pierce, and David).

each curve indicates the intensity of the masking tone.

When considering more than two tones, the masking effects change as the overall intensity changes. Harvey Fletcher, a pioneer in psychoacoustics, did experiments in this with the following results. With a complex sound of 400, 300, and 2000 Hz of respective intensities of 50, 10, and 10 db, the 300-Hz tone was completely masked and only the 400- and 2000-Hz tones were heard. However, when the intensities of all three were raised by 30 db to respective levels of 80, 40, and 40, then the 2000-Hz tone was completely masked and only the 400- and 300-Hz tones were heard. This provides more good evidence that, for correct reproduction, sounds and music should be recorded at the same intensities at which you intend to play them back. It also stresses the importance of monitoring sounds in the studio at the same levels you intend for playback, particularly if you are concerned with equalizing or filtering the sound.

When the ear is exposed to a masking sound, there is, as we have just noted, a rise in threshold. If the masking sound covers a broad band of frequencies, the threshold shift will occur throughout the audible frequency range. If the masking sound is of any duration, the threshold shift will not disappear immediately when the masking sound is removed, but will be reduced gradually over a period of time. This phenomenon is known as *auditory fatigue,* and the masking sound, in this case, is sometimes known as the fatiguing sound. The longer and louder the fatiguing sound is, the longer and more severe will be the fatigue. When the ear is exposed to extremely high intensity levels, the rise in threshold can be permanent, meaning partial deafness. All this must be considered when setting levels of sound cues in the theatre. Levels that are too high could cause temporary or permanent damage to the hearing of either the actors or the audience, depending on who is close to the speakers. Levels that will not cause damage but that are, nevertheless, quite high will cause auditory fatigue lasting anywhere from a few seconds to half a minute. This means that whatever sound follows in that time span may not be fully perceived or comprehended, particularly if it is an actor speaking. (The frequency range generally considered to be essential for comprehending speech extends from about 1000 Hz to 2500 Hz, and this is the range that is most likely to suffer fatigue from anything but strictly high frequency sound effects.) A constant bombardment of fatiguing sound can put an audience in a very bad frame of mind and present a difficult obstacle for actors to overcome.

AESTHETICS AND PSYCHOLOGY

Drama is part of what is known as "the performing arts." In order to know where sound design fits into the theatrical scheme aesthetically, we must first examine, briefly, the aesthetics of theatre in general. In everyday existence our senses become very economical and selective, choosing to sense only those objects and feelings that are necessary for the purpose of the moment; and even then we do not perceive those objects and feelings fully, but only superficially to the extent to which they are momentarily useful. (As I go toward my couch to sit on it, I see a gold couch; I generally do not see the play of light and shadow on it as the plants above it sway in the breeze from the open window. As you read this book, if you are concentrating properly, you are probably not fully perceiving the background noise around you—that is, you would not be able to say how many cars drove past or how many birds chirped while you read this paragraph.) When we go to a theatrical performance we know that the life situations on the stage are not actual but only virtual (appearances of actual situations). Our only purpose for the time we are there is to take in the theatrical performance. This frees our senses from the economy and selectivity necessary for dealing with actual situations and enables us to experience fully the sensations and feelings that are excited by the theatrical situation.

The life situation is a process of suspense and resolution, balance and unbalance, a rhythmic movement from moment to moment as the resolution of one tension becomes the beginning of another. The rhythmic pattern is fast and unending; there is usually little time to think about or appreciate one experience because you are already into the next. The theatrical situation, however, can focus on one particular object or emotion or experience and in that way can abstract it from actuality and heighten the sensation or feeling of it. In the theatre we can stretch a momentary situation, both in duration and in tension. We can isolate it in time and space from all other experience, so that the audience can perceive this one experience fully. But this focus, this stretching and isolating (and therefore abstracting) of an experience, is done through the interacting and blending of many different elements (speech and movement of actors, costumes, scenery, lights, and sound). And these elements must be perfectly blended for the illusion and the tension to hold. If the individual physical elements show through as such, the piece, as a work of art, breaks down.

Sound is one of these physical elements. Its functions are many. It can be used to expand time and to heighten tension during expanded time. It can begin or end a rhythmic segment of time, or lead from one segment to another, providing continuity. It can be used to diffuse momentarily the focus and concentration or, at other times, to pinpoint focus and concentration. It can provide a tempo and an aural texture for a scene and suggest a mood. But whatever function it serves it must always remain an integral part of the production as a whole. The sound score cannot be self-serving. No individual sound can be humorous or frightening or however effective except as it relates in that manner to the situation on stage. If you include sounds just because they are, say, funny in and of themselves, then whatever illusion you are trying to create on stage will be broken.

In psychological terms, a sound effect is not meant to provoke an emotion as an isolated stimulus but only as it relates to the theatrical situation. Sounds themselves do not have emotional qualities; there is no such thing as a happy sound or a sad sound. Some sounds do provoke emotional reactions not related to the immediate situation, but they are usually general and most often are related to the memory of a previous situation. A very loud, sharp sound will startle a person and may evoke a brief period of fear until the sound is identified and classified in the mind. The feeling of fear may continue after identification if the sound is recognized as coming from a source of danger; but this is related to previous experience and is a learned response. A sound may be humorous, but only as it is recognized as a distortion or mockery of another sound. Some sounds may evoke a feeling of peace and contentment, but these sounds are usually associated with past experiences in which the sound was associated with a peaceful setting. (Such nature sounds as a brook flowing through the woods, a gentle breeze rustling the leaves, and waves gently lapping the shore are a case in point. These sounds, in fact, have now become conventional for evoking feelings of peace and contentment, and recordings of them are sold to be played as background sound for calming stressed nerves.) So we can see that many realistic sounds can evoke an emotional response or create a prevailing mood because they are recognizable and can be associated with past experience. (Even then, individual responses will differ according to individual experience. The usually calming sound of waves lapping the shore may evoke a negative response in a man whose wife was drowned in the ocean.) The use of abstract sounds to evoke a particular emotional response is more difficult, since there is usually no association with past experience and the response must be made solely in terms of the current experience. On a secondary level, a sound that is a direct abstraction of a realistic sound may evoke the same emotional response as that sound or may evoke a response in relation to that sound. In the theatrical situation, a sound is used either to establish a mood (by the use of a sound which conventionally has association with that mood) or to evoke an emotional response in relation to the immediate situation. The exact same sound can evoke two entirely different responses depending on whether the immediate situation is comic or dramatic.

In the course of this book we have studied what sound is; how it is created, recorded, and reproduced; and how it can be used to enhance a theatrical production. The first, acoustics, is a science; it is based on facts and formulas. The second, sound engineering, is a skill and, if you will, a craft; it can be acquired with practice by anyone so inclined. The third, sound design, is an art, or at least one aspect of a collaborative art; it demands an understanding of that art as a whole and a definite point of view from the artist. It is hoped that in the course of time the student who begins as a craftsman in the field of sound will become an artist in that field as it relates to the theatre.

GLOSSARY, SYMBOLS, AND ABBREVIATIONS

AMBIENCE—the acoustical characteristics of a room or environment in which sound is reproduced. An ambient or live room is one in which a sound will produce some reverberation.

ANECHOIC—refers to an environment in which a sound produces absolutely no echo or reverberation. This can be either high up in the air over an open plain (with no mountains or city buildings to reflect sound) or in a specially built "anechoic chamber" in which the walls and ceiling are constructed and treated so as to absorb rather than reflect sound. These chambers are used for testing speakers, and the environment is sometimes referred to as "free-field."

ATTENUATION—the lowering in strength of an audio signal. When you turn *down* the volume control on a mixer or amplifier you attenuate the sound. The volume control is called an attenuator.

CHANNEL—the discrete path of an audio signal through a sound system. In terms of a simple stereo system there are two separate channels that go from the sound source (turntable or tape deck) through the system and out the two speakers, and are never crossed or mixed. In a theatre sound system, however, there are usually many "input channels" (paths that go from the sound sources—tape decks, turntables, or microphones—*into* the mixer) and several "output channels" (paths that go *out* of the mixer and through amplifiers to speakers). In any case, the word "channel" refers to the signal path which, through any specified section of a system, is kept isolated from any other signal path.

CONCEPT—usually used in theatre to describe the unifying ideas of a physical production; what makes that production of a particular play different from any other production of that play. Some examples of production concepts are: *A Comedy of Errors* set in the Old West; *Hamlet* set in Washington, D.C., in modern dress; *Macbeth* done à la spaceships and creatures from outer space (poor Mr. Shakespeare seems to be on the losing end); *You Can't Take It with You* done in black and white like an old television show and using radio-type sound effects.

CROSSTALK—signal leakage between two channels; the opposite of separation.

DAMPING—the reduction of mechanical or electrical resonances.

DISCRETE—separate, isolated. In

terms of theatrical sound, discrete refers to sounds that are recorded through different channels onto different tracks and are kept entirely separate from each other even though they run parallel on one tape. They may then be played back through different speakers in the theatre or, even if they are mixed together and played through the same speakers, they may be controlled by separate volume controls.

DRY—refers to an original audio signal before any distortion such as reverberation or equalization has been added. "Dry" may also refer to an audio signal that has little or no natural ambience.

GAIN—a volume control on any piece of audio equipment.

GENERATION—a dub or copy of a tape, referring to the number of times a sound is rerecorded. (A third-generation tape is a copy of a copy of the original.)

MONAURAL (MONO)—refers to a single-channel recording or a single-channel system or piece of equipment.

QUADRAPHONIC—refers to a four-channel recording, system, or piece of equipment.

SELF-SYNCHRONIZATION—a feature on some multitrack tape decks that allows the monitoring of a previously recorded track from the record head (instead of the playback head) while recording on another track. This means that there is no time difference between what is heard from the two tracks, and the track that is being recorded can be synchronized exactly with what is already on the tape.

STEREOPHONIC (STEREO)—refers to a two-channel recording, system, or piece of equipment.

TRACKS—the parallel but separate areas of recording on a tape, or the areas of the heads that record or play back. (See Chapter III for a full explanation and illustrations.) Tracks should not be confused with channels: tracks refer strictly to the recording configuration of the tape heads or of a previously recorded tape; channels refer to the paths of the audio signal through the mixing and amplification stages of a system or the amplifier section of a tape deck.

AM—amplitude modulation—see Chapter I.

cps—cycles per second, unit of measure of frequency; see also "Hz."

db—decibel, unit of measure of sound intensity—see Chapter I.

f—frequency—see Chapter I.

FET—field effect transistor—see Chapter III.

FM—frequency modulation—see Chapter I.

Hz—Hertz, unit of measure of frequency—see Chapter I.

ips—inches per second, unit of measure of tape speed.

λ—(Lambda) wavelength—see Chapter I.

LED—light-emitting diode—see Chapter V.

mic—microphone.

Ω—(Omega) ohm, unit of measure of impedance—see Chapters II and III.

pot—potentiometer, device used for attenuating sound.

rpm—revolutions per minute, unit of measure of turntable speed.

Z—Impedance—see Chapters II and III.

APPENDIX II – WIRING DIAGRAMS

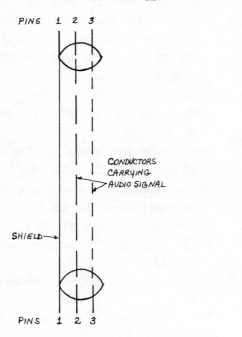

A. WIRING FOR 2 CONDUCTOR SHIELDED CABLE INTO
3-PIN CANNON CONNECTOR. (FOR LO-Z,
BALANCED MICROPHONE.)

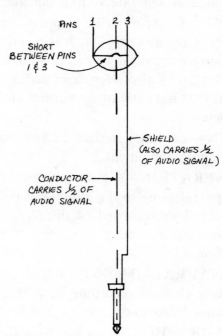

B. ADAPTER FOR GOING FROM SINGLE CONDUCTOR
SHIELDED (UNBALANCED) TO THREE PIN CANNON
CONNECTOR.

APPENDIX Ⅱ - WIRING DIAGRAMS

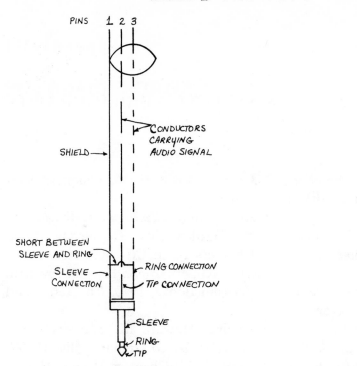

PINS 1 2 3

CONDUCTORS
CARRYING
AUDIO SIGNAL

SHIELD

SHORT BETWEEN
SLEEVE AND RING

SLEEVE
CONNECTION

RING CONNECTION

TIP CONNECTION

SLEEVE

RING

TIP

C. ADAPTER TO GO FROM LO-Z BALANCED MICROPHONE
INTO LO-Z UNBALANCED INPUT.

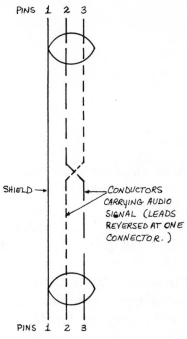

PINS 1 2 3

SHIELD

CONDUCTORS
CARRYING AUDIO
SIGNAL (LEADS
REVERSED AT ONE
CONNECTOR.)

PINS 1 2 3

D. ADAPTER OR PATCH CORD FOR REVERSING THE
PHASE OF A MICROPHONE OR MIXER OUTPUT.

A SELECTED BIBLIOGRAPHY

(After each work is indicated the chapters of this book to which the work is relevant.)

Beranek, Leo L. *Acoustics.* New York: McGraw-Hill, 1954. Chapters I and IX.

Burroughs, Lou. *Microphones: Design and Application.* Plainview: Sagamore, 1974. Chapters II, III, and V.

Kinsler, Lawrence E., and Frey, Austin R. *Fundamentals of Acoustics,* 2d ed. New York: John Wiley & Sons, Inc., 1962. Chapters I and IX.

Langer, Susanne K. *Problems of Art.* New York: Charles Scribner's Sons, 1957. Chapter IX.

Meyer, Leonard B. *Emotion and Meaning in Music.* Chicago: University of Chicago Press, 1956. Chapters VIII and IX.

Pierce, John R. *Electrons and Waves,* rev. ed. Garden City: Doubleday, 1964. Chapters I and IX.

Taylor, Rupert. *Noise.* Harmondsworth: Penguin Books, 1970. Chapters I and IX.

Tremaine, Howard M. *The Audio Cyclopedia,* 2d ed. Indianapolis: H. W. Sams, 1973. Chapters II and III.

van Bergeijk, Willem A., Pierce, John R., and David, Edward E., Jr. *Waves and the Ear.* Garden City: Doubleday, 1960. Chapters I and IX.

Weitz, Morris. *Problems in Aesthetics: An Introductory Book of Readings.* New York: Macmillan, 1959. Chapter IX.